THE MAKING OF LIVERPOOL

'THE MAKING OF ...' Series

'The Making of ...' series is a new collection of local histories, brought to you by Wharncliffe Books. This series is not intended to be a chronological account of each area, but instead it highlights the prominent factors, which bring to life the development and character of a town, city or area. These highly illustrated books contain illuminating snapshots captivating the history and nostalgia of the locality.

The Making of Manchester, Mike Fletcher • 1 903425 32 8 • £9.99
The Making of the South Yorkshire Landscape, Melvyn Jones • 1 871647 53 6 • £9.95
The Making of the West Yorkshire Landscape, Anthony Silson • 1 903425 31 X • £9.99
Published November 2003

'ASPECTS' Series

With over 32 books currently available in Series, 'Aspects' books are unique in that they allow many local authors and historians to contribute articles to each volume. Articles are made up from a collection of nostalgic and historical pieces relevant to an area, each of which is highly illustrated.

Aspects of York, Alan Whitworth • 1 871647 83 5 • £9.95
Aspects of the Yorkshire Coast, Alan Whitworth • 1 871647 54 1 • £9.95
Aspects of the Yorkshire Coast 2, Alan Whitworth • 1 871647 79 7 • £9.95

'FOUL·DEEDS AND SUSPICIOUS DEATHS' Series

Each book will take the reader into the darker side of their town or region; covering stories that once shocked, horrified and captivated the people who lived there. From the strange to the macabre, to murder and mystery, the authors examine those cases, analysing both motive and consequence, alongside the social conditions prevalent at the time.

Foul Deeds and Suspicious Deaths in Blackburn & Hyndburn, Stephen Greenhalgh
1 903425 18 2 • £9.99

Foul Deeds & Suspicious Deaths In and Around Chesterfield, Geoffrey Sadler
1 903425 30 1 • £9.99

Foul Deeds & Suspicious Deaths In and Around Rotherham, Kevin Turton
1 903425 18 2 • £9.99

Foul Deeds on the Yorkshire Coast, Alan Whitworth
1 903425 01 8 • £9.99

Foul Deeds & Suspicious Deaths In and Around The Tees, Maureen Anderson
1 903425 07 7 • £9.99

Foul Deeds & Suspicious Deaths in Wakefield, Kate Taylor • 1 903425 48 4 • £9.99

Forthcoming 'Foul Deeds ...'

Foul Deeds and Suspicious Deaths In Leeds, David Goodman
1 903425 08 5, £9.99, Published September 2003

Foul Deeds and Suspicious Deaths In and Around Durham, Maureen Anderson
1 903425 46 8, £9.99 Published October 2003

Foul Deeds and Suspicious Deaths in Nottingham, Kevin Turton
1 903425 35 2, £9.99, Published October 2003

More Foul Deeds and Suspicious Deaths in Wakefield, Kate Taylor
1 903425 48 4, £9.99, Published November 2003

Please contact us via any of the methods below for more information or a catalogue.

WHARNCLIFFE BOOKS
47 Church Street • Barnsley • South Yorkshire • S70 2AS
Tel: 01226 734555 • 734222   Fax: 01226 734438
E-mail: enquiries@pen-and-sword.co.uk • Website: www.pen-and-sword.co.uk

The Making of
LIVERPOOL

Mike Fletcher

Series Editor
Brian Elliott

Wharncliffe Books

First Published in 2004 by
Wharncliffe Books
an imprint of
Pen and Sword Books Limited,
47 Church Street, Barnsley,
South Yorkshire. S70 2AS

For up-to-date information on other titles produced under the
Wharncliffe imprint, please telephone or write to:

    Wharncliffe Books
    FREEPOST
    47 Church Street
    Barnsley
    South Yorkshire S70 2BR
    Telephone (24 hours): 01226 - 734555

ISBN: 1-903425-53-0

A CIP catalogue record of this book is available from the
British Library

Front cover illustration: *Lord Street, c1908.* Author's collection
Rear cover illustration: *The Mersey Tunnel, c1930s.* Author's collection
Contents page illustration: *Castle Street, c1900s.* Author's collection

Printed in the United Kingdom by
CPI UK

Contents

$\mathscr{I}$NTRODUCTION

Liverpool is famous for many things: its port, its architecture, and its music. Its people are equally famous for their unique accent, a devastating humour, and a natural resilience in the face of adversity. It is this depth of character that makes Liverpool's story such an interesting one. *The Making of Liverpool* attempts to capture the essence of that history by highlighting the great changes in the life of Liverpool and its people.

Although created by King John in 1207, the name Liverpool originates from the Norsemen that settled on the banks of the Mersey during the tenth century, using an inlet, known as the Pool, as a natural harbour for their long-ships; they called this place *Lifrig*, and it is the later corruption of the terms, *Lifrig* and *Pool*, that gave us the name Liverpool.

Liverpool has had a chequered history – and at times a violent one: coming under siege on three occasions during the English Civil War. During the Georgian era Liverpool was a boom town, which not only embraced the Industrial Revolution, but led the transport revolution too; pioneering the creation of turnpikes, river navigations, canals and railways in Lancashire, and developing a world famous port that gained the title *Gateway to the West*. Such progress came at a price, however, and Victorian Liverpool was filled with such high levels of poverty, deplorable housing and crime that it acquired the nickname *The Black Spot on the Mersey*.

During the twentieth century Liverpool has witnessed poverty, destruction during two world wars, the Mersey Beat and the Beatles which placed Liverpool on top of the world in the 1960s, and high unemployment, dereliction and despair, as its traditional industries suffered decline during the 1970s and 1980s, and the city took on a more aggressive role, reflected in the Toxteth Riots of 1981 and the rise of Militant Tendency.

In more recent years Liverpool's fortunes have begun to improve. Today, Liverpool is a city reborn, a vibrant city, intensely proud of its heritage and culture, and yet excited about its future. It is this new-found confidence that ensured it won the title *European Capital of Culture 2008*. There's a great deal of hard work still to be done, but over the next five years Liverpool will regenerate its international image in time to revel in glory during 2008, a worthy capital of culture!

$\mathcal{A}$CKNOWLEDGEMENTS

The North-West of England is blessed with a host of excellent local studies libraries and record offices, and this book could not have been written were it not for their invaluable assistance. I would like to thank and pay tribute to the staff of Liverpool Record Office, the Lancashire Record Office, the Local Studies Unit of Manchester Central Library, the Local History Library & Archives of St Helens and Warrington, respectively, and Preston's Harris Reference Library. Each of these bodies holds a massive amount of relevant information on the history and development of Liverpool and its hinterland through the ages.

The photographs used in this volume either come from my own collection, or have been taken by me for the purposes of this book. However, I would also like to thank Bob Dobson of Landy Books for locating some of the wonderful engravings and illustrations, and also V & C Finn of Rainford for supplying some of the interesting picture postcards.

Last, but not least, I would like to thank the staff of Wharncliffe Books for their support and encouragement throughout this project – in particular Barbara, Sylvia, Sue and series editor Brian Elliott.

$\mathcal{W}$AR & REBELLION: LIVERPOOL'S VIOLENT PAST

1

Liverpool has had a very violent past. On many occasions it has seen war and rebellion on its doorstep. Its very creation was as a direct consequence of rebellion. An uprising had begun in Ireland during the early years of the reign of King John, and the king was anxious to quell it. Unable to use the existing north-west ports of Milford Haven and Chester because of his enemies, the king was forced to create a new naval port, and chose the River Mersey, and the shelter of the natural harbour known as the Pool.

The Borough of Liverpool was created at a stroke with the passing of a charter in 1207 and the king then established a naval port from which to attack the Irish; and to protect this from any possible attack the king ordered that a new castle be built. Sadly, there is no surviving record of when construction of Liverpool Castle actually began, but it was only fully completed by 1237. By all accounts the castle was a

This commemorative picture postcard, printed in 1907 to celebrate the 700th anniversary of Liverpool's charter, shows Aethelflaed, Queen of the Mercians and daughter of Alfred the Great, who granted Ingimund, leader of the Norsemen, land on either side of the River Mersey during the tenth century. From this originates the name Lifrig-Pool, *or Liverpool.* Author's collection

Elfleda
daughter of Alfred the Great
riding from Runcorn Castle

This, another of the commemorative picture postcards from 1907, depicts the granting of the charter by the much-maligned King John, to form the borough of Liverpool on 28 August, 1207, offering 200 burgages with the individual rent of 1s per annum. Author's collection

bold fortification, built on the headland overlooking the Pool, and encircled by a huge moat, cut from the natural rock. Within its five foot thick ramparts, entered by a bold gate house with a barbican located at the north tower, were two large courtyards, divided by a curtain wall, one of which contained a well that was covered by a wooden structure referred to as the 'House'. It had three tall, impressive towers, the largest of which was the west tower, which housed the Keep and the Great Hall. The chapel stood below the south tower and the armoury was housed in the third and final tower. The castle was of a good size for the period, with its east wall measuring 38 yards, the north wall 36 yards, west wall 35 yards and the south wall 37 yards.

Today, the castle's former location is occupied by Victoria's Column, overlooking the Law Courts. The Pool, which once passed alongside, and stretched as far as Whitechapel, was filled in during the eighteenth century. An orchard and dovecote led from the rear of the castle down to the river – which today are completely covered by Lord Street.

The Banastre Revolt

Liverpool Castle was used on several occasions through the years as a symbol of power and authority in the region, but the first time it came under attack was in 1315, during a localised dispute which led to the Banastre Revolt.

Thomas, Earl of Lancaster, who had succeeded his father some years earlier, was proving to be much less a man than his father had been. His greatest supporter was Robert De Holland, a ruthless character who craved power, using Thomas' weakness to his advantage. De Holland's oppression of Earl Thomas' subjects had severe consequences, however, and ultimately led to the Banastre Rebellion of 1315. Adam Banastre of Shevington, supported by William Bradshaigh of Haigh, gathered his forces on the outskirts of Wigan and from there led his rebels on a merry rampage throughout the region.

They attacked many symbols of Earl Thomas' powerbase, including Liverpool Castle, an obvious symbol of power in the region, though failed to break its defences and had to make a graceful withdrawal. Undeterred, they crossed the Mersey and attacked Halton Castle at Runcorn, breaching its defences by burning down its gates. Later, they turned their attention to Manchester and

In order to protect the new settlement, King John ordered that a castle be built - Liverpool Castle - on high ground overlooking the Pool, and encircled by a huge moat, cut from the natural rock. It was an impressive fortification, with ramparts five feet thick, and three tall towers. Throughout the years many artist impressions have been created of Liverpool Castle - this is one dating from the end of the eighteenth century. Author's collection

Trafford Hall, before moving on to Preston. It was here that the rebels' merry dance came to an end, finally meeting their match, when a superior force, commanded by De Holland and the Sheriff of Lancashire, brought the rampage to an end. This was a time of local unrest in the region, and fearing that other similar revolts might occur, King Edward II actually visited the area the following year to act as a calming influence, staying in the safety of Liverpool Castle.

Influential Families and Territorial Feuds

There were many prominent families within medieval Liverpool, all with ancestors that had 'crossed the channel with the Conqueror, and, having played a significant role at Hastings, had been rewarded by the king with land. The two most influential families were Stanley and Molyneux, each aspiring to even greater status, and both having a great rivalry over the other, which often led to violent disputes.

Of the two families, the Stanleys had come from more humble beginnings. Initially called De Audley, the family had been granted land in Staffordshire, settling in a village called Staneleigh which by the reign of Henry III they had adopted as their surname: William de Audley, grandson of Lord Audley, is thought to be the first member of the family to call himself William de Staneleigh. Throughout the years, their surname would be further corrupted to the more familiar spelling of Stanley.

The Stanley's gained greater status through marriage, first acquiring the manor of Storeton, Cheshire, which also gave them the title, Bailiff of Wirral Forest; subsequent marriages led to the family owning all of the Wirral Peninsula. By far the most significant boost to the family's status came with the marriage of John Stanley and Isabel de Lathom in 1385, which brought massive influence, land and property, including Lathom House, Knowsley Hall and Liverpool Tower. John Stanley found favour at court too, and Henry IV made him Lord Lieutenant of Ireland. Such was Stanley's position that when he seized the Isle of Man in 1404 the Crown did not interfere; in fact the following year the king made Stanley Lord of the Isle of Man. In 1406 the king granted Stanley the right to fortify the Tower of Liverpool. From this point onwards, the Stanley family held massive power and influence within Liverpool: up until that time they had been referred to as '...a family of the Wirral' – thereafter they were referred to as the 'Stanleys of Liverpool'.

The Mollines family had also shown great valour at Hastings and had been raised to a position greater than that of the Stanleys, having been awarded land at alongside the River Alt, including the manors

An artist's impression of medieval Liverpool from the River Mersey. Liverpool Castle dominates the town to the right of the picture. Moving from right to left, the Town Hall can be seen, whilst on the high ground stands Everton Beacon, a guide to shipping for many years, and in the bottom left-hand corner, St Nicholas Church and Liverpool Tower. The fact that Liverpool had two fortresses - the Castle and the Tower - and two rival families - the Stanleys and Molyneux - meant that trouble was bound to occur! Author's collection

of Sefton, Crosby and Great Crosby. Richard de Mollines was the first lord of the manor, his descendants became Constables of West Derby Castle during the twelfth century, and later Constables of Liverpool Castle. During the thirteenth century they changed their family name to Molyneux.

Through the years the feud between the prominent families of Stanley and Molyneux had become legendary, and by the early years of the fifteenth century matters had reached boiling point. William de Stanley was attacked on the ferry, between Birkenhead Priory and the Port of Liverpool, on 23 August 1414, by a gang of around 200 men, led by Sir Henry Norris of Speke, and Richard Bold of Bold (both were known supporters of Molyneux). Matters continued to escalate: in the summer of 1424, the Molyneux family massed a force of around 2000 and prepared for an all out attack on Liverpool Tower; the Stanleys mustered around 1000 men and prepared to repel the attack. The inhabitants of Liverpool feared that a civil war was about to take place in the streets of their town: some took sides and prepared for battle, others wanted none of it and took to the safety of their homes. In the end, trouble was only averted at the last minute, and peace restored, by the intervention of the Sheriff of Lancashire, on behalf of the king.

Ship Money

Although the accession of Charles I had resulted in Liverpool acquiring a new charter, it also brought with it many unpopular measures. The call for ship money to be levied against the town in 1634 annoyed many in Liverpool. The fact that Liverpool, a naval port, was being charged £25, a figure considerably less than its comparable neighbours (Wigan and Preston each paid almost twice as much), seemed to have escaped the attention of the council. They took on a militant tone, and, led by the uncompromising figure of Edward Moore, flatly refused to pay! This attitude did not endear the people of Liverpool to the king.

The English Civil War: Liverpool Under Siege

As the growing divisions between king and Parliament escalated into civil war, each town began declaring for either King or Parliament. Liverpool declared in favour of the king, and was seized with apparent ease and without resistance, by James Stanley, Lord Strange, for the Crown.

James, son and heir of William Stanley, sixth Earl of Derby, had already taken on the role and duties of his elderly father, and would lead the Royalist forces within the region. In September 1642, Lord Strange opened the hostilities within Lancashire, leading his Royalist Army against Manchester, to seize for the Crown the arms and gunpowder he himself had stored there. Although the Manchester Siege resulted in failure for the Royalists, and deep personal embarrassment for Stanley, it was here that he received the news of his father's death and that he was now the seventh Earl of Derby.

Although the north-west Royalists enjoyed some victories in the early stages of the war, as time went on it was evident that the Parliamentarians were better organised, directing their forces from their Manchester headquarters, and slowly the tide turned in their favour, as the Royalists lost control of town after town. By May 1643, much of Lancashire was within Parliamentarian control, and Liverpool was one of the few remaining Royalist strongholds.

The First Siege of Liverpool

With the fall of Warrington, Wigan and Preston, the Royalists knew that Liverpool must surely be next on the Roundheads' list. The town was vulnerable to attack, particularly as the Royalists were in no shape militarily to defend it. However, the first siege of Liverpool, although expected, came from a most unexpected quarter.

In another of the 1907 commemorative postcards, we see Liverpool Tower. This had been a traditional home of the De Lathoms, and had passed into the control of the Stanley family following the marriage of Sir John Stanley and Isabella de Latham. Permission to fortify the house had been granted in 1406 by King Henry IV. It would remain in the Stanley family until the execution of James, seventh Earl of Derby, in 1651. Author's collection

The Royalist army had been outflanked at Whalley, south of the Ribble, and were now on the run. Lord Molyneux ordered the Royalists into a retreat, taking them south-west through to his native Liverpool, rapidly pursued by a superior Roundhead force, commanded by Colonel Assheton. Fearing imminent capture, Lord Molyneux fled across the river into Cheshire, while the remainder of his weary army took safety within Liverpool Castle. Colonel Assheton, seeing his enemy cornered, ordered his forces to surround both the town and castle. The first siege of Liverpool had begun.

This siege, proved to be short-lived. Following two days of very intense fighting, the Roundheads mounted a powerful attack on the Royalists' defences, and succeeded in breaching them. Their attack was co-ordinated and calculated: the Roundhead troops advanced along Dale Street, capturing Liverpool Tower and St Nicholas' Church, and securing the town, before finally turning their attention to the castle. With such a massive onslaught, the

Royalists were simply overwhelmed, and the Roundheads soon victorious. It was a massive defeat for the Royalists, sustaining heavy losses: 90 were killed, almost 400 severely wounded, and around 300 horses were captured.

Immediately following their victory, the Roundheads spent the intervening period fortifying both the castle and the town's defences. They summoned the support and expertise of Colonel Rosworm, the German military engineer whose skill and superior knowledge of defences had saved Manchester during its earlier siege. Rosworm oversaw the excavation of a huge defensive ditch excavated around the outskirts of the town, and a huge embankment forming a defensive rampart, stretching from the river, along Oldhall Street and Dale Street to link up with the end of the Pool. (Interestingly, at the end of the war, with the fighting over, this ditch was back-filled, only to reappear in the early decades of the twentieth century, by way of subsidence in Dale Street.) A regiment of horse and foot were rapidly summoned from Manchester to help reinforce the captured town. Liverpool's inhabitants were also forced to enlist – those that refused were heavily fined – and all suspected Royalist sympathisers were expelled from the town.

The Second Siege Of Liverpool

By now the Parliamentarian campaign had been so thorough that the vast majority of Lancashire, and indeed much of the North West, lay within their grasp. There were, however, a couple of notable exceptions: Lathom House, located between Ormskirk and Wigan, and Greenhalgh Castle on the outskirts of Garstang; both were properties owned by the Earl of Derby, and both were now under Parliamentarian siege, though the occupants were proving to be resilient. With the Earl still hiding on the Isle of Man, the Roundheads, commanded by Alexander Rigby, under the overall control of Sir Thomas Fairfax, felt that Lathom House was for the taking. However, they had seriously underestimated the resourcefulness of the Countess of Derby, a formidable lady, who, it was remarked, 'commanded her forces as well as any general'. Despite being offered a negotiated surrender, and promise of safe passage for both her and her children, the Countess refused, and through resourcefulness outwitted the Roundheads on several occasions. Despite her fortitude, as the siege dragged on, the Countess realised that in spite of their successes and sheer determination, they could not hold out indefinitely, and so a messenger was despatched, smuggled out during the night, and sent 'with God's speed', to

Castle Street is one of Liverpool's oldest streets, and formed the central bar of the letter H during the formation of the town's early streets. As the street outside Liverpool Castle, throughout the years this street has witnessed much bloodshed. During the many periods of trouble – from the Banastre Revolt, to the three sieges of Liverpool – the attacking forces would have used this street to approach the castle. If only streets could talk, what an interesting tale they might tell. Author's collection

summon support.

The Roundhead commanders were all too aware that a rescue force would surely arrive to free Lathom House, and this assumption proved correct. Prince Rupert, nephew of King Charles, led a superior force of men north in May 1644. Although he planned to free Lathom, his overall intention was to relieve York, for if this could be achieved then the Royalists might begin a fresh campaign in the region.

Rupert's advance was swift, crossing from Cheshire to Lancashire across the River Mersey (via the ford at Hale, to avoid passing through Parliamentarian-held Warrington), he was subsequently joined by the Earl of Derby. And yet, even before they reached Lathom, the combined Royalist armies received news that the siege had ended, with Alexander Rigby and his Roundheads fleeing rather than go up against the advancing Royalists. Upon hearing this news, Rupert ordered his army to attack Bolton – one of the towns in the region loyal to Parliament. This would prove to be a decisive move, for the Roundheads that had besieged Lathom had fled there days earlier.

Medieval Liverpool had many influential families: the Stanley's, Molyneux, Crosses, and of course, the Norris's of Speke Hall - today it is Liverpool's oldest and most famous residence, hidden away alongside the city's Liverpool John Lennon Airport. Author's collection

The consequence was that this battle, which had personal overtones for the Earl of Derby, led to the notorious Bolton Massacre.

James Stanley, Earl of Derby, now convinced the Prince that if a new front was to be established within Lancashire, then it was imperative that Liverpool be recaptured. Rupert agreed, and, after securing Bolton, the Royalists proceeded west to Liverpool to retake the castle for the Crown.

On 9 June 1644, Rupert's forces, amounting to some 10,000 men, assembled around Everton Beacon, a high point from which to view the town. Looking down upon Liverpool, Rupert himself is said to have described the town as 'a mere crow's nest' and easy for the taking. Forming his headquarters at a tiny cottage at Everton, it later gained the nickname 'Rupert's Cottage'.

Prince Rupert positioned artillery on the hillside, and spread his forces along the ridge overlooking the town (today that 'hillside and ridge' has long since been levelled, and is occupied by St George's Hall and Lime Street). From here they launched their initial attack, but

it was repelled by the Parliamentarian defences. On several more occasions, over a period of five or six days, the Royalists attacked the town but without success; for despite the ferocity of these attacks, they were easily repulsed by the Roundheads heavily defended behind Rosworm's superior fortifications. Prior to the siege commencing, the Roundheads had summoned more men, and had sent away women and children from the town. Nevertheless, heavy casualties were inflicted on both sides, though the Royalists suffered the worse of the two; losing around 2000 men in just one encounter.

It was obvious that a different strategy was required, and Prince Rupert enlisted the local knowledge of Lord Molyneux and his brother, Caryl. Together, they surveyed the defences and found a breach, where the ramparts joined the Old Hall. They launched a night assault on the town on 14 June, from the dense woodland of Kirkdale. Entering through the breach, under the cover of darkness, they took the inhabitants completely by surprise in the early hours of the morning. This was a bloody battle, and by far the

Liverpool had been created as a naval base, but it would develop as a port. By the close of the medieval period and throughout the Tudor reign, the port gained favourable status, trading with Ireland, the Isle of Man, France, Spain and Portugal. This illustration, painted in 1797 by S F Serres and later engraved by W Floyd, depicts Liverpool's ancient waterfront. Author's collection

largest amount of casualties, inflicted upon both sides came that night; hundreds were slain, buried the following day in shallow, unmarked graves. When the Royalists finally secure the castle, they discovered that Colonel John Moore had fled, by sea, on board his ship, taking his garrison with him. What few Roundheads that had survived the intense battle were imprisoned in Liverpool Castle.

The massacre that had occurred in Liverpool that night, which included civilians, although not on the scale of what had occurred earlier at Bolton, would be something that the inhabitants of Liverpool would neither forget or forgive. Also, during this successful attack, Prince Rupert seized the Common Council's records, along with Liverpool's medieval seal; which was never returned and a copy had to be made.

Following their victory, the Royalists placed Sir Robert Byrom in charge of Liverpool Castle, with a small force of men. Prince Rupert remained in Liverpool for just a couple of days before leading his army through Ormskirk and Preston, and crossed the Pennines to free the besieged town of York on 19 June. This proved to be a fateful campaign, resulting in the famous defeat on Marston Moor. It has been said that the determined defence of Liverpool had weakened the Prince's position, causing him to use an excessive amount of men and munitions to capture it; a lack of munitions that had implications for the outcome for his subsequent defeat on the Yorkshire Moors.

The Third and Final Siege Of Liverpool

Despite his army's defeat on Marston Moor, Prince Rupert successfully escaped death on the battlefield and fled, accompanied by Captain Chisenhall (who had served in the siege of Lathom House) back to Lancashire. Fairfax desperately wanted the Prince captured, and despatched an expeditionary force of one thousand men in pursuit. Although these men were diligent and thorough in their search, the Prince evaded capture, and seemingly managed to slip through their fingers.

The remnants of the defeated Royalist army crossed back into Lancashire, fleeing down the Ribble Valley and crossing the River Ribble at the ancient ford at Freckleton, just west of Preston. Upon reaching the opposite bank they plundered their way through Hesketh Bank, continuing into North Meols, where it is claimed they terrified the locals.

Sir John Meldrum had been leading a force of Roundheads in pursuit, but were prevented from crossing the river by the incoming tide. Another Roundhead force, commanded by Colonel Assheton, who had been camped at Hesketh Bank, picked up the chase. Maintaining the pressure, they forced the Royalists to vacate the coast and head inland. Although the Royalists made a stand at Aughton Common, near the market town of Ormskirk, they were routed by the combined forces of Assheton and Meldrum, causing them to retreat to the safety of Liverpool Castle. It is interesting to note that in later years, musket shot and cannon balls have been discovered around Hesketh Bank and Crossens, as well as at Aughton itself.

This was a bleak period for the inhabitants of the region, for apart from having to contend with the fighting and continual bloodshed occurring on their doorsteps, the dreaded plague had returned once more. Warrington was one of the first towns to fall victim to this outbreak, and its close proximity to Liverpool so terrified the burgesses, that they instigated a curfew, and a watch on all the roads leading to Liverpool, preventing any strangers entering the confines of the town. Thankfully, in this instance, Liverpool was spared a visitation from this killer disease. However, it was not spared further bloodshed.

Looking at this postcard of the 1930s, featuring the entrance to the Queensway Tunnel, its hard to believe that during medieval times and up until the beginning of the eighteenth century that this was the far end of the Pool, which stretched along both Paradise Street and Whitechapel. Author's collection

The third and final siege of Liverpool began in August 1644 and lasted through to November. This was a classic blockade: Colonel John Moore employed ships at his disposal to blockade the mouth of the Mersey, to prevent supplies or reinforcements reaching the besieged Royalists trapped in the castle. The combined Roundhead force was commanded by Sir John Meldrum, who chose to play the waiting game. For rather than shed needless lives in vain attempts to attack the castle, he held his position and starved the captives into submission. The Earl of Derby made a valiant effort to free Liverpool, though his forces were beaten back.

Lathom House also came under a second siege in 1644, though this lacked the romanticism of the previous siege. Both Liverpool and Lathom were eventually starved into surrender, and this effectively brought the conflict in the region to a close.

However, the peace lasted less than four years, and would be shattered in 1648 with the start of the second campaign. This conflict was short-lived and bloody, beginning with the Battle of Preston, where Cromwell's New Model Army defeated the English Royalists, commanded by Sir Maraduke Langdale, and ended with the final defeat of the Scots Army led by the Duke of Hamilton, at Red Bank, near Winwick. Although with hindsight it is clear to see that this second campaign was limited to the centre of the county and so left Liverpool and its residents alone, at the time its direction was uncertain and the Parliamentarians in Liverpool, fearful that they would be attacked, readied the town for the worst. When news arrived that the Royalist campaign had been defeated, they stood down again.

The final attempt to reinstate the Stuarts came in 1651, with Charles II leading an army from Scotland, joined by Colonel Thomas Tyldesley and the Earl of Derby. This force suffered its first defeat at Wigan Lane, and its final defeat at Worcester. On each occasion, the Earl escaped the battlefield; though he was finally arrested in Chester, and was executed in Bolton later that year for the part he played in the massacre of 1644.

After the wars, the actions of the Liverpool people were rewarded by the Lord Protector, who had, like many, realised that they had aided, albeit indirectly, in the victory over the Royalists on Marston Moor. Cromwell made the Port of Liverpool independent in 1658. Liverpool Castle, regardless of an order issued by Parliament to raise it to the ground, survived through to 1670, when it was considered surplus to requirements, and was partly demolished and left in ruins.

The Glorious Revolution

The death of Charles II in 1685 and the succession of his younger brother James, a known Catholic, had divided both the nation and Parliament. Fears that Catholicism would be reinstated ultimately led to the Glorious Revolution of 1689, and the ousting of King James in favour of William of Orange and his wife, Mary, daughter of King James.

King James had not fought for his throne, but instead fled to France, where he raised an army, before crossing to Catholic Ireland to gather greater support there, ahead of any invasion of the mainland. King William, fully aware that should James land an army on the mainland he would be supported by the disgruntled Catholics, raised an army and departed London on 4 June 1690, arriving in Liverpool seven days later.

Once again, Liverpool was a hive of military activity. Here, the king gathered munitions and stores, and assembled more men prior to crossing the sea to Ireland, landing at Carrick Fergus on 14 June. The uprising in favour of King James would be short-lived. On 12 July, the two forces met at the River Boyne and it was here that any hope that King James had of recovering his throne were dashed.

Unfinished Business

In spite of Liverpool's concentration on world trade, through the expansion of its port and the construction of its first docks during the early years of the eighteenth century, as far as others were concerned, civil struggle and political wrangling, common during the previous century, were far from over.

Although Britain had been united with Scotland, following the *Act of Union* in 1707, the wrangling of the Stuarts and their supporters was far from settled. They had been enraged by the Glorious Revolution of 1689, and the accession of William of Orange. And within Lancashire, the anger amongst the Jacobites was to prove wholly destructive. Here, members of prominent families met in secret to discuss this unhappy situation, many just grumbled amongst themselves, though others took the matter a might more seriously.

At Standish Hall, just north of Wigan, William Standish, a known Jacobite, gathered together other like-minded people: amongst them were several members of prominent Liverpool families, including William Blundell of Crosby, Sir Rowland Stanley of Hooton on the Wirral, and most prominent of all, Lord Molyneux of Sefton. The members plotted the assassination of the king, and the reinstating of James II. This later became known as the Lancashire Plot of 1694, and all were arrested and taken for trial in Manchester; they were later acquitted, due to the lack of credibility of the chief prosecution witness, John Lunt. Although some breathed a sigh of relief, many in Liverpool were not in favour of the Jacobites, and felt angry that the conspirators had apparently got away with treason.

The accession of Queen Anne had settled some of the plotting by the Jacobites, but her death in 1714, and the accession of George I, Elector of Hanover, rekindled the anger once more. The majority of the inhabitants of Liverpool, most notably the Earl of Derby, supported this new royal family; however others, most notably Lord Molyneux, did not.

The Jacobite rebellion of 1715 spread fear in Liverpool that its port might come under attack from the rebel army, and led to calls for the castle to be fortified. Since its partial demolition following the end of

The first siege of Liverpool did not last too long, as the Roundheads mounted a powerful and co-ordinated attack, advancing along Dale Street, capturing Liverpool Tower and St Nicholas Church, prior to securing the castle. This picture postcard of Dale Street dates from the late Victorian period, and its impressive array of buildings betray its commercial heritage. Author's collection

the civil war, the castle had been partly rebuilt when it housed King William's garrison prior to his departure to defeat James II in Ireland, now the Common Council issued funds for it to be reinforced and garrisoned to repel any Jacobite landing. When the rebellion came a cropper at Preston, Jacobite prisoners were transported to various Lancashire towns, including, Lancaster, Wigan and Liverpool, for trial and subsequent execution. Liverpool executed four prisoners on Gallows Hill (the location of London Road today).

In the immediate years following the rebellion Liverpool Castle was once more abandoned and left derelict, and made to look all the worse when it was inhabited by vagrants. It would remain in this sorry state through to 1721, when it was completely demolished, to make way for the construction of St George's Church, completed in 1734.

The '45 Rebellion

In 1745, thirty years after the first Jacobite rebellion, a more serious attempt by the Stuarts was made to retake the English throne. Britain was at war with France, and the Government was distracted, its reserve forces busy guarding the southern regions in case of an attack from across the channel. Seizing the moment, Charles Edward Stuart (Bonnie Prince Charlie to his supporters, the Young Pretender to his enemies) landed in the Outer Hebrides, and gathered vast support in Scotland, raising a rebel army and leading them south to London.

In Liverpool, the merchants, who had grown prosperous under the Hanoverian reign, greatly feared this invasion and the damage – both structural and economic – that it would surely cause. They felt vulnerable to attack, for their castle lay in ruins, and since the Civil War the army had disbanded, apart from regional garrisons: the nearest of these was Chester, leaving Liverpool completely undefended. The Common Council called an emergency meeting, and voted unanimously to form a local militia, donating finances for its armament, thought to be in the region of £5,000. The Council petitioned the Government for the right to form this militia, which was granted. In a short space of time, over 1,000 men had joined up, forming a force known as the Liverpool Blues, commanded by Colonel William Graham. Once assembled, the regiment received orders to depart Liverpool and head through to Warrington: the authorities believed that the Jacobite army would cross the Mersey here, and so this was to be the line of resistance. When, in the November, the Jacobite's had reached Lancaster, the Liverpool Blues were ordered to begin destroying the bridges across the Mersey.

When the Jacobite rebels reached Wigan, fearing attack might be imminent, the Liverpool Common Council gave orders that women and children should be sent across the river to the Wirral, where they might be safer. The shops and some of the houses in Liverpool were boarded up, and the remains of gunpowder and munitions were put onboard ships out in the Mersey. Under the orders of Prince William, Duke of Cumberland, all of Liverpool's vessels were 'put under the protection of his majesty's ships of war'. Their fears proved to be without foundation, however, for the Jacobite rebels were heading directly for London, and would never come any closer to Liverpool than Wigan.

Once the rebels had departed Manchester and continued south to Derby, the Liverpool Blues were ordered to link up with the approaching Hanoverian Army, commanded by Prince William,

Duke of Cumberland.

Upon hearing the news that this army, and another commanded by General Willis, was advancing upon them, the Jacobites retreated, retracing their original route, through Manchester, Preston, Lancaster and on to Carlisle, where they left the Manchester Regiment, commanded by Colonel Towneley, to defend Carlisle Castle, while the Prince and the Scottish Army crossed the border into Scotland. Although the Manchester men put up a brave fight, they were outnumbered by the combined force of the armies of the Hanoverian's, including the Liverpool Blues. With the threat of invasion over, the men of Liverpool returned home, and were disbanded in January 1746.

The failed rebellion had not only dashed the hopes amongst the Catholic population, but had raised anti-Catholic feeling to a new level. At the end of April an angry mob gathered in Liverpool and attacked the Catholic chapel of St Mary. In the following month further riots occurred and several Catholic homes were vandalised. This time the authorities had to act and the military were summoned and soon dispersed the mob.

2   THE TRANSPORT REVOLUTION

The Hanoverian age would witness the genesis of the Industrial Revolution. However, despite the quite radical changes that occurred in the manufacture of goods, equally important was the radical transformation in transport. The Industrial Revolution desperately needed to be mobile, it needed the transportation of not just raw materials, but the completed articles, otherwise the revolution might well have simply withered on the vine. In Liverpool's case, a town that had remained isolated throughout the centuries, it needed to be linked to an efficient transport infrastructure. In the short-term, however, what it desperately needed most of all was the reliable transportation of coal to power its furnaces. During the Hanoverian era, a transport revolution occurred in which Liverpool was at the forefront.

The River Navigation Age

Liverpool, compared to other emerging towns in the region, had always been at a disadvantage when it came to transport, an isolated community, it lacked the accessibility of other Lancashire towns. Its riverside location had been its saviour. The Mersey ferries, linking Liverpool to Cheshire, had begun in medieval times and had kept busy. Hamo de Massey, Baron of Durham, granted the Benedictine monks the land at Birkenhead for them to build their Priory, and they in turn established the ferry service. However, the Mersey, in those times, was a turbulent river, subject to tidal changes, and without the defences built in much later times, in bad weather it would have been a most hazardous crossing, so the monks felt duty bound to charge for the service. Prior Robert de Waley had petitioned King Edward II for the right to erect buildings on the foreshore, on either side of the Mersey, where lodgings and food could be arranged, and received a charter on 20 November 1317; but the service was not officially recognised until the charter of 1330. Following the Dissolution, the service passed through many owners: initially to Ralph Wolscy, then to the Corporation of London, of all places, before being purchased by a man named Poole, who had lived in the township of Sutton (later part of St Helens). The ferries provided an important connection between the two counties throughout the seventeenth century.

By this time, however, as transport became all the more important, and if Liverpool was to really excel and not get left behind, it would need to invest in superior links to other towns within the county. The river had been its principal means of transport, and for many years, the concept of creating a navigable waterway between the towns of Liverpool and Manchester, had been debated. Even as early as 1660 the subject had been approached, with a proposal that the rivers Mersey and Irwell could be made navigable. However, although a navigation Bill was prepared and placed before Parliament, it failed. In this pre-industrial era, the River Mersey was a clean river, with clear flowing waters and salmon locks along its length between the Runcorn Gap and Warrington. In the following centuries the Mersey would witness a massive explosion of industry which would pollute its waters.

The first workable navigation of the River Mersey came about in 1694. Thomas Patten of Warrington installed weirs and locks to raise the water level and make it usable for flats and barges to reach his copper works at Bank Quay. Although this had involved some minor navigation work, it was not a navigation in the true sense of the word, with much of the success relying upon the tide passing up the river from Liverpool. Nevertheless, so successful was Patten's waterway that he proposed to extend it through to Manchester, by navigating the upper reaches of the Mersey as well as the River Irwell. Unfortunately, regardless of his overwhelming enthusiasm, Patten would never complete this task.

Liverpool was an isolated town, surrounded by marshland which was difficult to cross even in good weather. Its saviour was its position on the River Mersey. Since the seventeenth century, there had been suggestions of improving the river connection by navigating the upper sections of the Mersey, and the River Irwell, so that Liverpool could be connected to Manchester. However, the Mersey & Irwell Navigation would not be fully completed until 1734. Author's collection

Liverpool was not alone in its quest for navigable waterways. Prior to 1700, Cheshire salt refineries had been built, located at Frodsham and Hale. So important was the transportation of salt to these refineries that Sir Thomas Johnson had pioneered the concept of making the River Weaver a navigation in 1696, a project that was to be jointly funded between Liverpool merchants and Cheshire salt men. The work was surveyed and a Bill created, which was placed before Parliament in 1709; it was rejected. A second Bill, incorporating several key changes, was proposed six years later, but received similar treatment. Undeterred, the promoters continued to lobby Parliament and the third Bill was finally accepted, becoming an *Act of Parliament* in 1721. Work was delayed for a few years, but finally got under way, and the navigation was completed in 1732.

In the meantime, the question of Liverpool's navigations still circulated. Thomas Steers, Liverpool's first dock engineer, proposed the navigation of the rivers between Liverpool and Manchester in 1712. He carried out a detailed survey of the route later that year, and produced a workable plan, which included the construction of nine weirs and eight locks designed to regulate the water level, and the dredging of sections to make the river deeper. Such were the advantages of a navigable waterway to both Liverpool and Manchester, that the concept was financed by a group of around forty like-minded merchants, including Thomas Patten, and a Bill placed before Parliament in 1720. At this time, river navigations were really coming into the fore, and Parliament had become enthusiastic towards them, and so raised no objections.

Although the Bill received the Royal Assent in 1720, work on constructing the navigation did not commence for another four years. Progress was slow, and it would be a further decade before goods could pass through to Manchester unhindered. This navigation, compared to others that Steers had been involved in (such as the Douglas or Weaver), was poor in design and fraught with problems – problems that were to plague it for many years. For example, where later projects would use selective cuts to reduce or eliminate the natural meanders in the river, this navigation did not. This meant that boats had to negotiate the more winding parts of the river, slowing their progress. Although Mersey Flats sailed along here, the navigation also had a towpath so crafts could be pulled along by horses. In spite of its many faults, the Mersey & Irwell Navigation would be the first workable link between Liverpool and Manchester, and as such increased trade dramatically between the two towns.

Thomas Steers' talents as an engineer were in high demand, for apart from working on the Mersey & Irwell and Weaver navigations, he was also asked to survey the possibility of navigating the River Douglas between the coal mining town of Wigan and its connection to the River Ribble at Tarleton, in 1712. Although Steers completed the survey, a disagreement between him and some of the major investors, caused him to decline the position of chief engineer, though he did maintain an advisory role.

Construction of the Douglas Navigation would be fraught with difficulties, both structural and financial, and it was not fully completed and open to traffic until 1742. Obviously, the question arises – just what interest could a navigation, linking Wigan and the River Ribble, possibly be to the merchants of Liverpool? The answer is coal. Liverpool was desperate for coal to operate its industry, and the opening of the Douglas Navigation linked it to the collieries of Wigan, in particular the Orrell Coalfield. Barges, laden with coal, sailed along the navigation through to the River Ribble at Tarleton. From there they supplied a versatile market which included Preston, Ireland and Liverpool.

Industrial Turnpikes

Even by the beginning of the eighteenth century, as far as usable roads were concerned, Liverpool was an isolated community, surrounded by poor marshy land, that was difficult to cross even in good weather, but near impossible in bad weather. Warrington, its nearest neighbour, was barely accessible – the ground was so boggy that carts could not cross it, so visitors risked a difficult and often hazardous journey on horseback or on foot. There were few roads to Liverpool – apart from the 'King's Highway' connecting Liverpool, Ormskirk and Preston – and the vast majority of these in a poor state and responsible to no-one.

Basic highways had existed throughout the centuries, but only during the prosperous Tudor era did the question of improving the overall state of these roadways first arise. The passing of the *Highways Act* of 1555, was the first piece of legislation that addressed the concerns of merchants and travellers alike. The new law made parishes responsible for repairing their roads on an annual basis, the legislation enforced with the threat of fines or imprisonment. And yet, these roads were still far from being satisfactory, with no recommended width, and no regular pattern of repairs, which meant potholes appeared and reappeared. Wet weather meant that the roads just washed out and would remain that way until the next time of repair. Traffic – horses, carts and pedestrians – churned up the roadway, which was often just soil; stone paving was, in some cases used to try and prevent this, some early causeways remain within parts of Lancashire today to offer some proof to the use of stone slabs. Roads and streets within the towns were treated differently. In the case of a borough such as Liverpool, these roads were repaired directly by the Common Council, who kept them in order for the free use of its citizens.

By the eighteenth century, as Liverpool struggled to become a serious trading port, and industry looked to settle there, the problem of linking the town with the remainder of Lancashire became a major issue. The salt trade was expanding in Cheshire, initially with brine extraction, though later with rock salt. Both of these needed refining into commercial salt, and a new establishment had recently opened on Liverpool's waterfront.

Unfortunately, Liverpool was hampered in its desires to be an industrial centre, for it lacked the main source of fuel for the emerging industries – coal. Despite its best endeavours to locate this resource on its own land, it was forced to look elsewhere. Prescot was the nearest town on the South Lancashire Coalfield, but transporting it the few miles to Liverpool was a huge problem. The makeshift road between Liverpool and Prescot was notorious for its poor condition, filled with pot-holes so deep and so wide that carts became stuck in them, and the ground so sodden that the roadway completely washed out in the wet winter months. The prospect of transporting a heavy cargo such as coal along it must have been a nightmare. In the early days teams of around thirty packhorses were employed to carry the coal from Prescot Hall Colliery through to Liverpool, but even these hardy animals found it difficult to negotiate these dirt track roads. Supplies were erratic, and clearly matters had to change.

The Common Council petitioned Parliament in 1725 for the right to construct a turnpike connecting the towns of Liverpool to Prescot. This application proved successful, finding support in Parliament and receiving Royal Assent on 26 July 1726. A committee was formed to both operate and control the turnpike, consisting of sixty-one trustees, who held their first meeting in May of the following year, and the project was awarded a twenty-one year lease. The land was surveyed and work commenced soon after. The initial turnpike was a simple, though reliable affair, which had three sets of gates where the tolls were collected: the main gate at Page Moss, a second at Roby, and a third and final gate at Twig Lane.

This was one of the first industrial turnpikes in the country, certainly the first in Lancashire, though it was also used by the travelling public. There were certain exemptions to the paying of the tolls, one of which was for worshippers on Sundays, and another was to locals living along or near the turnpike who used sections only; after all it was the through traffic that the Trustees wanted to charge.

The rising cost of coal from Prescot by the 1740s led to calls for an extension to the turnpike so it might reach the coal mining town of St Helens. This gained parliamentary approval and the turnpike reached St Helens in 1746. Further extensions followed, linking Ashton in Makerfield in early 1757, and shorter extensions were subsequently added linking Old Swan and Huyton. The *Act* of 1757 also allowed the Trustees to create a further turnpike from Prescot through to Warrington, via Rainhill, Bold and Great Sankey. Further roads followed. In 1770 an *Act of Parliament* was passed for the construction of another turnpike route, from Liverpool to Preston, via the market town of Ormskirk, following the line of the King's Highway. This was a significant route for Liverpool, for at Preston it linked with other turnpikes, providing connects to other important towns, such as Lancaster and Carlisle.

The extension of the turnpike, from Prescot through to the St Helens, in 1746, enabled Liverpool to access the town's productive collieries. Prescot Road follows the line of that turnpike, and on the outskirts of St Helens, the district of Toll Bar, pictured here, confirms the former site of a toll gate. The Author

The Age of the Stagecoach

Although the turnpikes had begun to assist the movement of goods, by the middle of the eighteenth century, as further sections of turnpike roads were added, a reliable network of roads, passable throughout the year regardless of the weather, began to emerge. This meant that for the first time, a reliable stagecoach service could operate without fear of potholes and other obstacles spoiling the journey. In fact, so poor were the roads prior to this point that there was only one carriage in the whole of the Liverpool area – owned by a former mayor, John Clayton, a wealthy and influential merchant, who had purchased Liverpool Tower.

On 26 September 1757 the post travelled by stagecoach between Liverpool, Ormskirk and Preston. By 1760, Liverpool's first coach services began operating between local towns such as Warrington and Manchester. In the following year a regular service, the *Flying Machine*, was travelling between Liverpool and London. Departing the *Golden Fleece* on Dale Street, it could take as long as four days for passengers to reach London. Later, as the stages and roads continued to improve, this was reduced to just two days; by the nineteenth century the introduction of fast coaches such as the *Umpire* and *Express* meant that the travelling time was within one day.

As more staging inns were opened new routes were created to a host of destinations. Stages between Liverpool and Prescot began to operate a regular daily service in 1767, and soon after the residents of Liverpool had sustainable links to places like Birmingham and Lancaster, and even across the Pennines to destinations such as York, Leeds and Hull.

The Sankey Brook Navigation

The new town of Liverpool, and its industries needed coal to operate. As the demand for coal grew the ever-increasing tolls on the turnpikes made the cost double by the time it reached Liverpool. Clearly, something had to change. River navigations had proved the best means to transport heavy cargoes such as coal, and so a similar navigation, linking the St Helens collieries to Liverpool, would have been the ideal solution to their problem. The major flaw in that solution was the fact that there wasn't a river running through St Helens – however, there was the Sankey Brook, could this be made navigable?

The Liverpool Common Council held a meeting on 5 June, 1754, when they came to the conclusion that the navigation of the Sankey Brook ought to be investigated, and instructed two engineers, John

The increasing tolls on the turnpikes, doubling the price of coal between St Helens and Liverpool, led to the creation of the Sankey Canal. Although it was passed as a navigation act the Sankey is a canal in every sense of the word. This photograph shows the final section of the original cut, towards the Gerard's Bridge terminus: it is very overgrown and the Rainford Brook now runs along the canal bed. The Author

Ashton and Henry Berry, to carry out a survey. The navigation of a brook had never been attempted before, but Berry, Liverpool's chief engineer, having just completed the construction of the Salthouse Dock, was the best man for the job. Ashton, a member of the Council and a merchant was there primarily to oversee the work.

Berry's survey was thorough, though the outcome was less than encouraging. Berry had lived in St Helens as a boy and knew the Sankey Brook well enough to know that it could not be made navigable to an extent were it could cope with traffic throughout the year. A navigation of the brook simply wasn't feasible; and yet, the success of this project was vital to the continued supply of coal to Liverpool. The only solution to this dilemma was a compromise: an arterial canal could be cut all the way from the River Mersey, near Warrington, through to St Helens. However, this solution was fraught with problems, not least of all that Parliament would never allow the construction of a canal: they had rejected a similar proposal in March

The construction of the Sankey Canal was a huge feat of engineering, using eight single locks and one double lock - later referred to as the Old Double Lock. Although the Sankey Canal inspired the construction of others, such as the Bridgewater Canal, and so effectively launched the canal age, it has not faired well through the years: in 1968 sections were filled in, and the Old Double Lock dismantled and altered into a 'staircase waterfall', seen here in this photograph. The Author

1754 between Leigh and Salford. The answer, therefore, was to construct the canal in secret. A Bill was put before Parliament for a 'Sankey Brook Navigation', and received the Royal Assent on 20 March 1755. Work commenced on 5 September.

This apparent deception to the true nature of the waterway, explains why the Sankey Canal was constructed in such secrecy; no publicity was released until its completion in 1757. The canal ran from an earlier short navigation near Warrington, between the River Mersey and Sankey Bridges, through the hamlets of Newton and Parr, until it reached its initial terminus at Gerard's Bridge, St Helens. In total the canal passed through eight single locks: the Sankey Lock connected it to the River Mersey, then the Bewsey Lock, Hulme Lock, Winwick Lock, Hey Lock, Bradley Lock, Newton Common Lock, Haydock Lock – and finally, a Double Lock at Parr; thereafter the canal maintained level progress through to the Gerard's Bridge terminus.

The Sankey Canal proved to be a complete success, vastly reducing the cost of transporting coal through to Liverpool via the Mersey. During the next few years several extensions were added. In 1762, two new extensions opened: one from Sankey Bridges to Fiddlers Ferry, where a superior lock to the Mersey, less affected by the tide,

The Sankey Canal was constructed using 'Liverpool money' to provide a reliable means of delivering coal. Originally the canal joined the River Mersey by a lock at Warrington, which was dependant upon the tide, and so the canal was extended and a new lock was opened at Fiddlers Ferry in 1762; in 1830, to compete with the railways, the canal was extended yet again and a new lock was built at Spike Island. The Author

had been built and the other from the Double Lock to Patten's new copper works at Blackbrook. In 1770, a second double lock – logically named 'the New Double Lock' was built on the section near Gerard's Bridge, raising the height of the canal, and taking it through to Ravenhead. The Sankey Canal achieved what it had set out to do: deliver a reliable supply of coal to Liverpool, and yet it also led directly to the development of industry at St Helens.

The success of the Sankey Canal put pressure on the owners of the salt mines in Cheshire to improve the existing Weaver Navigation, effectively making it a sea-going canal. The Cheshire salt merchants, together with the Liverpool refinery owners, complained that this was too inefficient and needed to be improved to cope with the increased trade. This improvement was begun by Henry Berry, but would be finally completed by Edward Leader Williams.

The Sankey Canal transported coal between St Helens collieries and Liverpool unhindered through to the nineteenth century. The birth of the 'railway age' in the 1820s brought competition. The opening of the St Helens & Runcorn Gap Railway in 1830 brought a rival means of moving the coal to the River Mersey, and so make matters equal, the Sankey Canal was extended to Spike Island by engineer Francis Giles later that year, where the two rival forms of transport had new docks side by side.

Canal Mania

Following the success of the Sankey Canal, other canals followed, such as the Bridgewater just two years later. Initially this waterway did not affect Liverpool, and the merchants of the town had no interest in it, that is until the Duke chose to cross the River Irwell (rather than lock down to it) and continue with his canal, both to Manchester, and more importantly, through Cheshire to Runcorn. When this extension opened in 1776, it became the first reliable sea-link that Manchester and Liverpool had ever had. Coal was transported along the Bridgewater Canal from Manchester to the industry at Liverpool.

However, the change of course of the Bridgewater Canal also meant that it could link with the Trent & Mersey Canal. Brindley had surveyed the route, in 1758, at the request of Lord Anson and Lord Gower, after Liverpool merchants had expressed interest in the idea of connecting the rivers of the Trent and Mersey by means of an arterial canal. Brindley's interest had come from a concept of creating a super canal, which he called the Grand Cross Canal, which could stretch throughout the country, connecting the major ports of

The creation of the Sankey Canal was vital to the continued development of Liverpool, but it also had a direct impact on the development of St Helens as an industrial town, boosting the colliery trade and attracting a variety of industries including glass, alkali and foundries working both iron and copper. These three photographs show the remaining section of the canal near St Helens town centre. The Author

Liverpool, London, Hull and Bristol. Unfortunately, this survey came to nothing as the proposed canal was dropped due to the high costs involved in its construction. It was resurrected again in 1765, when Josiah Wedgwood proposed that the rivers of the Trent and Mersey be connected by a waterway, so he could transport his pottery more efficiently: once again, Brindley was chosen as the chief engineer, following discussions with the Duke of Bridgewater. With its completion, Liverpool had, for the first time, reliable inland connections to the south.

The completion of the Duke's canal placed it in direct competition with the Mersey & Irwell Navigation; of course it had been the inadequacies of this navigation that had compelled Francis Egerton to construct his famous Bridgewater Canal. The canal was vastly superior to the river navigation, and so the proprietors of the navigation (knowing they could not compete) offered it for sale to the Duke, for £10,000: he rejected the offer.

The navigation was later sold to a group of merchants from both Liverpool and Manchester, who invested heavily in the improvement of the waterway, rebuilding the weirs and locks in stone, and installing cuts to reduce the more awkward meanders. A new section, called the Latchford Canal, was added to the navigation to improve the worse stretch between Warrington and Runcorn in 1804; and in 1824 a further cut, between Warrington and Rixton – known as the Woolston Cut – improved the passage of traffic greatly. Where the Mersey & Irwell Navigation did have the upper hand over the Duke's canal was on the size of its locks, these were much larger, allowing much larger vessels than the conventional barges to pass through to Manchester.

Within eight years, the arrival of the Liverpool-Manchester Railway brought with it increased competition, which led to a decline in the Mersey & Irwell Navigation, that could not stay abreast of the race for traffic. The Bridgewater Canal, on the other hand stood its ground well against its new rival, and would purchase the Mersey & Irwell Navigation in 1844.

The Leeds & Liverpool Canal

By the second half of the eighteenth century Liverpool now held a great deal of influence in the region, and was often consulted on new transport proposals. In 1766, for example, suggestions were soon being circulated that a new canal could be built to cross the Pennines and link the textile counties of Lancashire and Yorkshire. The proposed destinations of this trans-Pennine canal were the ports of

The coal mining town of Wigan was of great interest to the Liverpool Common Council, and they insisted that the Leeds & Liverpool Canal be re-routed to connect with the town. When the canal finally reached Wigan during the 1770s, warehouses and coal tippers were built at the original terminus - today known as Wigan Pier. The Author

Liverpool and Hull, but by December of 1768, that had been forgotten for a much more challenging project designed to link Liverpool with Leeds. This concept hoped to improve the links between the textile trades of Lancashire and Yorkshire, traditionally divided by the great mass of the Pennines, the backbone of England; which had to be crossed using teams of hardy packhorses, over land that was often impassable for long periods during the winter months.

Regardless of any 'grand scheme' to join Lancashire and Yorkshire together, to the members of the Liverpool Common Council, the main priority was still the continuous supply of coal; the more coalfields the new canal could connect to the better – and their primary interest was the coal mining town of Wigan. However, the original route of the Leeds & Liverpool Canal completely bypassed Wigan, instead taking a more direct route across Lancashire, between Ormskirk, Leyland, Chorley and Colne. The Liverpool Common Council were far from happy and even suggested withdrawing their interest in the venture in 1769. Matters wrangled on between the two parties.

The dispute over the direction of the Leeds & Liverpool Canal, and the Common Council's interest in greater connection to the Wigan Coalfield, soon fuelled speculation that rather than mess around with a massive undertaking of a trans-Pennine canal, would it not be simpler to construct a direct Liverpool-Wigan canal, which could even link with the Sankey Canal en route?

By now, Liverpool was a hive of alternative suggestions – such as the proposal of the South Liverpool Canal – leaving Liverpool from the south, shadowing the river, and again connecting with the Sankey, before continuing through Newton and Hindley and on to Wigan. Another suggestion involved the cutting of an extension to the proposed Leeds & Liverpool near Knowsley, from where it could travel through to Runcorn, where the proprietors of the Sankey Canal had pioneered the bold suggestion that an aqueduct could be built over the River Mersey at Runcorn, to connect both canals with the Bridgewater Canal. However, despite such overwhelming enthusiasm, all of these schemes would later be dropped, purely on the grounds of cost.

Even though these other ideas were circulating and gaining backing from some quarters, from the outset the principle that this new Leeds & Liverpool Canal would be created remained firm. Further negotiations between the merchants from both sides of the Pennines led to a new route being adopted. The canal would depart Liverpool from the north, passing through Burscough, Parbold, Appley Bridge and down into Wigan, and from there it would utilise part of the southern section of the Lancaster Canal through to Chorley, where a staircase of locks carried it up and over the moorland hills, through the mill towns of Blackburn, Burnley and Colne; and finally into Yorkshire.

With the route now finalised and agreed to by both parties, James Brindley was chosen as the surveyor, assisted by John Longbottom. The survey was carried out swiftly, and the investors were eager to sign Brindley as chief engineer, but he declined, due to pressure of work, and Longbottom took on the task instead.

The Bill was presented to Parliament in 1770, receiving Royal Assent later that year and construction commenced immediately of the 127 mile long waterway simultaneously at both sides of the Pennines. At the Lancashire side, the first sod was cut in a grand ceremony at Halsall, between Liverpool and Ormskirk, on 5 November 1770. Good progress was made, and by 1774 the Liverpool section had reached as far as the River Douglas Navigation at Parbold, and barges were already using the waterway. The canal took a long sweeping route through to Wigan for two good reasons, firstly it passed through areas of quarries, and second, this route maintained a contour line, which eliminated the need for too many locks. Nevertheless, the project was soon over budget, and worked ceased until the 1790s, due to lack of sufficient finances. In the meantime, Wigan's coal continued to be delivered to Liverpool's docks via the Douglas Navigation as far as Gathurst, where it joined the open section of the Leeds & Liverpool Canal at the Dean Lock.

Although the Leeds & Liverpool Canal had been the first of the trans-Pennine canals to begin, by the time of its completion in 1816 it had been beaten by both the Rochdale Canal and the Ashton Canal. Nevertheless, the waterway proved a great bonus to Liverpool's trade, transporting the much-needed coal; as it entered Liverpool several large coalyards opened along it length. It also typified the role that Liverpool played in the expansion of the Lancashire textile industry: raw cotton was transported from Liverpool along the Leeds & Liverpool to the mill towns of Wigan, Blackburn and Burnley.

Through the years the Leeds & Liverpool Canal proved to be a huge success. The opening of the Leigh Branch in 1816 not only linked it to the Bridgewater Canal – providing an alternative route between Liverpool and Manchester – it also gave access to the collieries of Leigh and Golbourne. However, the distance between the canal's Liverpool terminus and the docks had long been of concern to the Common Council, and as early as 1799 a proposal of connecting the canal directly to the Prince's Dock had found

The opening of the Leigh Branch of the Leeds & Liverpool Canal in 1816 was significant, for it enabled coal from collieries such as Maypole, Bickershaw and Parsonage collieries to reach Liverpool. The Author

support. However, internal wrangling prevented the proposal going any further until 1811. In that year the Common Council approached the canal engineer William Chapman, who produced a survey. Unfortunately, further wrangling delayed the project, and it was only in 1846, with the construction of a new section and a flight of locks, that the canal would be linked to Stanley Dock, thus providing immediate access to Liverpool's shipping.

Liverpool's transport connections to the south increased again in 1793, when an *Act of Parliament* gave permission to the Ellesmere Canal Company, to begin work on the canals to connect the rivers of the Mersey, Dee and the Severn, headed by their chief engineer, Thomas Telford. This great network of canals, which linked the port of Liverpool to the Midlands, became known as the Birmingham & Liverpool Junction Canal in 1826; later the Birmingham & Liverpool Junction Canal, the Ellesmere Canal and the Chester Canal united to form the Shropshire Union Canal.

The Effect of the Railways

The emergence of the canal network in the eighteenth century had greatly assisted Liverpool's growth and development as an industrial port. And, despite the arrival of the railways in the 1820s and their continued expansion, the canals continued to hold their own throughout much of the nineteenth century, particularly in the transport of coal.

Although the railways were initially seen as a rival and ultimately a successor to the canals, in many ways the railway companies proved to be the canals saviours, as almost all the canals would be bought out by the railway companies: the Sankey Canal was bought by the St Helens & Runcorn Gap Railway in 1846, and the Leeds & Liverpool Canal was leased by the LNWR during the 1850s. Although the Leeds & Liverpool Canal survives through to present day intact, and thrives as a medium for pleasure boating, the Sankey Canal, arguably the genesis of the canal age, lies in semi-dereliction, with large sections having been filled in during the 1960s.

3   *D*EVELOPMENT OF THE TOWN

The history of the Borough of Liverpool is one of slow development. There were times when, compared to its neighbours, Liverpool was progressing quite rapidly, and yet there were also many periods when it was in severe decline. However, from humble origins Liverpool would develop.

Development of the Medieval Borough

When history remembers the reign of King John it sees him as the bad younger brother of the good King Richard, the tyrant that was forced into the signing of the Magna Carta in 1215 by his barons, only to rebel and inflict misery and suffering on those that had coerced him into signing that restrictive document. And this is probably the most accurate image of him, and yet if it were not for the actions of the bad King John Liverpool might never have been created.

The Royal Borough of Liverpool was created on 28 August 1207 with a charter awarded by King John: granting a Royal Borough Seal, made of silver, depicting the eagle of St John the Evangelist. To create a town, the king offered 200 burgages with an individual rent of one shilling per annum. This was a great incentive, for the taxes here were substantially lower than in other, more established areas. Although the original charter did not give the right of the fee farm (to set and collect the local taxes), this was awarded later in the same year with a Letter Patent. Once the town had been established, further burgages were offered, around 180 in total, although they were not of the same standard as the originals. And so the Royal Borough of Liverpool had been created. Throughout the middle ages the county of Lancaster would have just four royal boroughs: Liverpool, Lancaster, Preston and Wigan. However, compared to its contemporaries, Liverpool was at a distinct disadvantage, as its location was isolated and it has to be said, less than perfect. The area surrounding the new town was boggy marshland, known as the Waste. Toxteth was heavily wooded and a royal chase. The nearest settlement was four or five miles away, again through heavy dense woodland, at West Derby.

As a medieval settlement, Liverpool established itself very quickly indeed. People found the river location attractive: the riverside was not only used as a naval port but was also home to a fishing fleet. Initially, the burgages were gathered around a single street, called the High Street. Shortly after, two other streets were added, leading up from the waterfront, called Chapel Street and Banke Street (today the two streets still exist, called Water Street and Tithebarn Street). Other streets were added to these three in a grid pattern, of an extended letter 'H' out from the river bank. Through the years, although the names of these streets are certainly changed, the basis of these still remains pretty much the same. Dale Street and North John Street are on the routes of the early streets. Castle Street, which also exists today, was added in 1237, with the completion of Liverpool Castle.

Castle Street's impressive heritage means that it is often referred to as 'Liverpool's most noble street'. At one end stood Liverpool Castle, which gave the street its name, and later, at the other end stood the Town Hall.

However, the death of King John and the succession of Henry III saw Liverpool's rapid expansion muted. Henry was less enthusiastic regarding Liverpool as a port and town, and he had no intention of developing its potential; instead he supported the continued growth and expansion of its rival, Chester. His refusal to grant Liverpool a new charter continued for thirteen years. In fact, in 1227, the king increased the toll he received from the town to 'eleven marks, seven shillings and eight pennies'. When the new charter was awarded, just two years later, the king had had a complete change of mind, and made Liverpool 'a free borough forever' and awarded them the right

This picture postcard, dating from the turn of the twentieth century, looks in the direction of the modern Town Hall.
Author's collection

of the previous charters, it withdrew the monopoly treasured by the burgesses of control and discretion they held over non-burgesses trade; which displeased the burgesses immensely.

Although Liverpool men had fought for the House of Lancaster during the early battles of the Wars of the Roses, the creation of the House of York in 1464 with the succession of Edward IV witnessed some restoration in Liverpool's fortunes, and the new king passed a new charter in 1468.

Tudor Liverpool

Liverpool developed into an organised town during the Tudor period, with a structure that would allow it to flourish in the new age. The grammar school was built in 1515, within the chapel of St Mary del Quay, following a significant donation from John Crosse of Crosse Hall, himself a chantry priest. Following the reduction of the chantries under the reign of Edward VI, the grammar school passed from church control to the local burgesses. Henceforth schoolmasters, and the decisions of the running of the school, were made by the Crown (as the Duchy of Lancaster).

John Crosse believed in the future of Liverpool, and donated sufficient finances for the construction of Liverpool's first town hall, which opened in the same year as the grammar school, occupying a site on Castle Street, at the opposite end to Liverpool Castle, the traditional boundaries of Liverpool and West Derby. Originally called the Exchange, it was often referred to as the Common Hall, as headquarters of the Liverpool Common Council. It was a simple two-storey building, with a thatched roof, containing offices on the first floor, reserved for the mayor, the borough court and the Common Council, with the ground floor being used as a warehouse and sales area for the trade of imported goods, and the cellars used as a prison.

By the accession of Henry VIII, although Liverpool's decline had been reversed and prosperity was gradually returning, it had its consequences: for the king now looked to increase the revenue he gained from Liverpool, and setting new tolls for non-residents entering the port, and bringing the control of the ferries within the claim of the Crown. King Henry also angered the burgesses by granting the fee farm to Sir William Molyneux, lord of the manor. Conflict between the lord and his burgesses was averted by a compromise being reached whereby the Molyneux would sublease it to the burgesses. By 1545, Liverpool was in a position where it could afford to return members to Parliament.

In 1556, the burgesses were granted the renewal of their charter by Queen Mary. And yet, in the following year the Molyneux family, lords of the manor, changed their minds and refused to renew the sublease; any crisis was averted by the intervention of the Earl of Derby. This action, if anything, increased the support that the Earl held locally, and further reduced that of Molyneux. Liverpool under the early Tudor monarchs was a better place than its medieval predecessor, the town more organised and much better run, and yet its population, at less than 700, was still recovering from the losses inflicted during the plague years of the fourteenth century.

Although the Elizabethan period would prove to be the most successful for the inhabitants of Liverpool, it did not begin too well, for the plague revisited Liverpool in 1558. This would prove to be a particularly severe outbreak. At the time Liverpool's population had just returned to the previous pre-plague levels, thought to be around 800, but this new outbreak was to spoil that achievement: deaths from the plague this time would reach almost 250, more than a quarter of the population! The inhabitants were heartily relieved to see the disease diminish and disappear, hoping that it would never return again – but, of course, it would.

The late-Tudor years would see many things: peace, war, plague, and local difficulties too. When Ralph Sekerston was appointed Mayor in 1560, one of his first duties was to call for the arrest of the previous mayor, Alexander Garnet, on the grounds that during his period as mayor he had refused to arrest a known criminal, Henry Clerck. Nevertheless, the term of imprisonment was not long, and neither did it affect his career, for he was elected as Mayor once more in 1565! Tudor mayors held greater power and influence than any other mayors before them. It was a demanding job, for apart from administering the running of the town, mayors had to audit the annual accounts, and inspect the borough boundaries once every seven years. As his volume of work increased, the mayor took on greater members of staff. He was also the judge during the meetings of the burgesses: which, without his intervention would have led to anarchy. During the reign of the Tudors, the office of mayor of Liverpool was filled by members of the Stanley family no less than eight times.

In 1565 Queen Elizabeth granted Liverpool the right to administer its chantries: this meant that for the first time, it could control the running of its own grammar school, appointing its own choice of headmaster for example; as well as the appointment of its priests. The burgesses now had almost complete running of the wealth and well-being of the town. By now the town was beginning to expand once more, and around half a dozen new streets were added within a couple of years.

The year 1580 was a turning point for the administration of Liverpool. Mayor Edward Halsall decided to appoint a permanent council of twelve aldermen, and twenty-four councillors, elected by the burgesses, to run the town: this was called the Liverpool Common Council. This was a significant change, for it meant that Liverpool now had self-determination, something that other towns – such as Manchester – did not. The Common Council later took over the fee farm lease from Caryl, Lord Molyneux, giving them complete control over the running and taxing of Liverpool. The Assembly, consisting of all of the burgesses, continued to meet, proposing matters for the council to rule on. Halsall, in an attempt to ensure that the members of the council, or councillors as they were later known, would be loyal, they had to swear an oath of allegiance.

By the end of the Tudor reign, Liverpool's overall appearance had changed only slightly; there had been some minor expansion of the streets, though ultimately it was still a settlement confined between the river and the Pool. Nevertheless, around Toxteth, the Royal Park had been disbanded, like so many other hunting grounds, and sections of land sold to locals; some minor construction had begun to take place too, though the vast waste was still just that. Throughout the Tudor reign, Liverpool's port had gained some favourable status, trading with Ireland, the Isle of Man, France, Spain and Portugal.

Stuart Liverpool

Liverpool's new-found trade and prosperity would continue throughout the reign of James I, yet it would be blighted by the turbulent reign of Charles I. The reign of King Charles had begun well for the people of Liverpool, with good trade established in the Elizabethan and Jacobean periods continuing. Against this backdrop of rising prosperity, Liverpool's burgesses had sought greater control of their own affairs, and had campaigned in vain to both Queen Elizabeth and King James I, for a new charter. And yet, following the accession of Charles I in 1625 Liverpool's case would finally be recognised, and the much awaited charter was awarded to the town on 4 July, 1626. This new charter was significant, for it offered the right of incorporation, and considerably extended the borough's powers with the right to form a council, stating that a 'mayor, bailiffs and burgesses had been incorporated'. This was somewhat ironic, as Liverpool had been electing its own town council since 1580, but this new charter gave it royal legitimacy.

The first mayor of the newly incorporated Borough of Liverpool, was James Stanley, Lord Strange, the son and heir to the Earl of Derby. Lord Strange, although a young man (becoming mayor just before his twentieth birthday), was already a powerful figure within the town, having been elected as its member of parliament the year before. He had fought hard to secure this charter, and would take his seat in the House of Lords in the following year, as Baron Strange.

The new charter also gave permission to elect aldermen, and the appointment of a town clerk. Unfortunately, the first person to hold the office of town clerk, a man named Dobson, chose to abuse his powers, bringing him into conflict with the mayor and indeed many other members of the council. Such was the hostility between them that Dobson's position was untenable and he was eventually dismissed.

Late-Stuart Liverpool

Although the years of civil war brought both death and destruction to the streets of Liverpool, the years following the Restoration in 1660 witnessed times of expansion. Liverpool broke away from its traditional H-shape street pattern and within a few short years many new streets were added to the town: Moor Street in 1665 and Fenwick Street three years later, are just two examples.

At the same time Liverpool was witnessing increasing trade through its port: the importation of cargoes such as linen and wool brought increasing wealth, as it traded with Ireland and the Isle of Man, which boosted the town's income and fuelled its expansion. Most of this new trade was largely due to the efforts of Sir Edward Moore (son of the disgraced Colonel Moore). And within twenty years of the Restoration, Liverpool's streets had increased to almost thirty: though this rapid expansion could not be sustained and eventually began to slow down, for within the following twenty years only another four were added.

Of Liverpool's many streets, the most contentious was that of Lord Street. The Molyneux family still retained the right of the fee farm lease, though were content to sublease this to the Town Council. However, further difficulties were just around the corner. In 1672, Lord Molyneux wanted to create a new street – Lord Street – running through his orchard, at the rear of the castle, and crossing the Pool to the Liverpool Waste via a bridge. Although by rights, the Liverpool Waste belonged to the lord of the manor, some years previous the burgesses had seized this land as their own. There was uproar amongst the council, and Liverpool's burgesses, angered that

In 1672 Lord Molyneux created a new street, from the castle through his orchard and down to the Pool, which he named Lord Street. The Pool ran along modern-day Whitechapel, and he caused uproar when he built a bridge over the Pool later that year: the mayor called for its demolition, but Molyneux negotiated, and both the bridge and his street remained. These two picture postcards show Lord Street as a busy thoroughfare in the second decade of the twentieth century. Author's collection

Lord Street, Liverpool. looking East.

This photograph of Lord Street and Whitechapel, taken in 1908, depicts the former location of that troublesome bridge! Author's collection

the lord of the manor could ride roughshod over their authority, decided upon direct action: the mayor immediately passed orders that the new bridge should be torn down. Molyneux wanted to keep his bridge, but rather than fight the council for it, he was prepared to negotiate: he offered the council the fee farm lease for a renewable term of one thousand years. The council agreed and the bridge remained in place. Later, the fee farm was purchased by the Town Council.

Liverpool was growing in stature in the latter years of the seventeenth century. Its original Town Hall was used until 1674, when a new building was commissioned. This Town Hall, or Exchange, was to be Liverpool's second public building, much larger and far grander than its predecessor, made of brick and stone, and standing on arches, under which the local merchants met. The upper floors were reserved for the Mayor, Town Council and other official meetings. The Customs House relocated to Moor Street (though later still, it moved to the waterfront, facing Stanley's Tower).

By the close of the seventeenth century the trials and tribulations that had befallen the town during the English Civil War were finally

It is hard to believe that Church Street, one of Liverpool's busiest streets, depicted here in the 1920s, was once part of an area of open heath and marsh referred to as the Liverpool Waste. It was only following the construction of the infamous Lord Street bridge that large sections of the waste began to be reclaimed. Author's collection

behind them, and Liverpool's overall status was certainly in the ascendancy. In 1698, for instance, seasoned traveller, Celia Fiennes visited the town and her observations offer us a snap-shot of how Liverpool was growing in stature and status, when she describes it as

> *a very rich trading town...the streets are fair and long* [with] *houses of brick and stone built high and even...an abundance of persons* [who are] *very well dressed.*

She went on to suggest that Liverpool was now 'London in miniature'.

Georgian Liverpool

Liverpool's continued expansion and refinement during the eighteenth century can be judged by Daniel Defoe's description of the town in 1712, when he stated that Liverpool was 'a large, handsome, well built, increasing and thriving town'. The new century would see Liverpool transformed into an international trading centre, with the expansion of the port, and the introduction of a superior transport infrastructure. Development was all around: the vast Liverpool Waste was also beginning to be enclosed, with strips of the new land being sold off to lease holders – and even prior to Steers, construction of Liverpool's first ever dock, parts of the upper section of the Pool had been filled in. At the turn of the eighteenth century there was a lot going on in Liverpool, and seemingly much for the residents to be proud. Within a matter of a few years the town would see the construction of several new churches. And yet this period was to see Liverpool's status as in independent town beginning to take shape.

Churches
The town's new parochial status, granted in the *Act* of 1699, had seen it sever its traditional ties with the parish of Walton on the Hill and the building of new churches within the town. Throughout the Georgian period a great many churches would be built within Liverpool.

Although St Nicholas' continued as the main place of worship within the town, it would now share the parish of Liverpool with a new church, that of St Peter, built in 1702 on the opposite bank of the Pool, in the design of Sir Christopher Wren's Holborn church of St Andrew. The total cost of constructing this new church would reach almost £3,000. Included in the 1699 *Act* it had stated that part of the cost ought to be borne by the parishioners by way of subscription, and so the sum of £400 was collected. St Peter's was consecrated on 29 June 1704.

However, Liverpool's rapidly expanding congregation led to the construction of a third church, St George, in 1726, on the former site of the medieval castle. It would take eight years to complete. This church would form an important landmark for Liverpool, and would remain in situ until its eventual demolition in 1899.

Liverpool's first church, created from the chapel of Our Lady and St Nicholas during the fourteenth century, was by the middle of the eighteenth century, looking rather jaded and a series of alterations and additions occurred. And yet Liverpool's religious need was far from being quenched. In 1748 St Thomas's church in Park Lane opened. Liverpool's St Paul's church was built in 1769: originally designed to have a dome that would have been as impressive as that of its London namesake, its design was simplified due to cost. In 1773, St Anne's opened on Great Richmond Street and in the following year St James's on Parliament Street. Although St John's was the last church built in Liverpool during the eighteenth century, during the later years of the Georgian period even more churches were erected, including St Mark in 1803 on Duke Street and St Luke at the top of Bold Street in 1811.

Eighteenth century Liverpool was blessed with many churches. The Church of Our Lady and St Nicholas had long been the main place of worship within the town, referred to as the sailors' church. It was the scene of an horrific accident in 1810, when the ringing of the church bells brought the tower crashing down, killing twenty-three girls from Moorfields School in the process. Following the Act of 1699 St Nicholas was joined by other churches, including St Peter in 1702, St George, built on the former site of Liverpool Castle in 1715, and later still St Michael.

Author's collection

Because of Liverpool being an active port, it has long been a melting pot for a variety of cultures and religions. Presbyterianism had been active in Liverpool since the middle of the seventeenth century. In the new century the movement continued to expand and new, larger chapels were built. The Castle Hey Chapel (later Harrington Street) had been commissioned in 1692, but was not built for another thirteen years. Two years later another chapel was built on Key Street, located off Tithebarn Street, which remained in use through to 1791, when an even larger chapel was built in Paradise Street. George Fox, founder of the Society of Friends or Quakers, had visited Liverpool in 1669. However, the first Friends Meeting House to be built in Liverpool arrived in 1711, located off Hackins Hey. This was occupied until 1791, when a new Meeting House was opened in Hunter Street. The Baptists had built their Meeting House the year before the Quakers, in James Street, and remained here until a chapel was created in Byrom Street in 1822. John Wesley, founder of the Methodist movement, visited Liverpool in 1775 and described it as being 'one of the neatest, best built towns in England'.

Greater Prosperity

The new Hanoverian age would lead to the move away from the traditional employment in agriculture, into manufacture, which brought increasing prosperity. Liverpool's flourishing port, together with its new transport links, meant that many businesses were attracted to the town. Business in Georgian Liverpool was expanding rapidly, and during the early years of the eighteenth century the town was busy with a variety of trades, including the construction of new salt warehouses, potteries, grain mills, sugar refining, rope-making, etc, and as commerce continued to increase money now poured into the town. This new wealth was evident for all to see, reflected in the in the amount of new buildings that were changing the look of the town's skyline. The merchants and businessmen of Georgian Liverpool built a town that was pleasing to the eye, with some of the grandest architecture seen anywhere in the world. And for themselves they built impressive rows of grand three storey terraced town houses, with magnificent façades of red brick, Portland stone porches and wrought iron railings, in areas of south east Liverpool, such as Toxteth, close enough to their investments but far enough away from the grime that was the rapidly emerging industrial Liverpool. Many of these Georgian houses still exist today and can be seen on Hope Street, Parliament Street, Canning Street – and Rodney Street, where, at No 62, William Ewart Gladstone was born, later prime minister to Queen Victoria on four separate occasions.

However, although Liverpool's merchants reaped the benefits of this new-found prosperity, Liverpool's poor did not, for rather than diminishing in number, they continued to multiply to alarming proportions. Their homes were extremely basic, huddled in damp courtyards, where several families might inhabit a single room. Unlike the grand Georgian homes of the rich that we see in Liverpool today, the hovels and slums of the poor have long since disappeared. It was during this period in Liverpool's history, however, that the poor and the working classes were beginning to be taken care of.

Schools for the children of the working classes were few and far between. The Bluecoat School was quite the exception when it was founded by William Blundell in 1717. All the pupils wore strict school uniform, consisting of a blue coat and hat. The workhouse, which opened next door to the Bluecoat School, in the appropriately named Workhouse Lane (though it later changed its name to School Lane) in 1732, was a grim place and the last resort of the poor and

Schools for the children of the working classes were few and far between. The Bluecoat School, created by William Blundell in 1717, was the exception and a huge step in the right direction. The school acquired its name because all the pupils wore strict school uniform, consisting of a blue coat and hat. The building, on School Lane, still survives today. Author's collection

The Hanoverian period witnessed many advances, such as the establishment of schools, dispensaries and other institutions, often funded by charitable donations from the more affluent members of society or the church. This engraving depicts Liverpool's Church School for the Blind on Duncan Street, which opened in 1819. Liverpool's poverty and poor public health was legendary. Its much-needed Infirmary opened on Brownlow Street, and tended to the poor free of charge. Author's collection

destitute of the town. Nevertheless, it would be extended in 1757 to cope with the ever-increasing poor of Liverpool. The introduction of the New Poor Law in 1834, in the autumn days of the Georgian period, made life within the workhouse that much more tougher. The welfare of the people of Liverpool was addressed with the construction of the Infirmary on Lime Street in 1748 (on the modern site of St George's Hall) and would be joined by the Seaman's Hospital four years later. The Church School for the Blind is a prime example for the greater care and attention that was being shown in Georgian Liverpool to the sick and the needy; designed by John Foster, the architect that had created St Luke's church, it was opened on Duncan Street on 6 October 1819 by the Bishop of Chester.

The growth of the town by the middle of the eighteenth century can be measured in a number of ways. A new charter was awarded by George II in 1752, which gave the mayor increased powers, and raised his status to Justice of the Peace. Liverpool's second town hall, located at the junction of the High Street and Dale Street, had been fighting a loosing battle with subsidence for a number of years: in 1740 one of its arches which had almost completely given way and had to be shored-up, and the elaborate turret was removed for fear that it might collapse. The grand old building finally succumbed to

Liverpool began to change quite significantly during the late-Georgian period, the streets of the town took shape, and shops and business were created. Bold Street became a place for the more discerning of Liverpool's population, with a variety of fine shops and ornate buildings, and it is due to this that it is often referred to as 'Liverpool's most pleasant street'. Author's collection

The Lyceum, on the corner of Bold Street, was built in 1821, at a cost of £11,000 paid solely by subscription by its 800 members. Its creation reflected the gentle image of Liverpool, with its news room and library frequented by the merchants. It still survives today as the Lyceum Post Office. Author's collection

its long-term problem of subsidence in 1748, when it was officially deemed unsafe by the council and condemned, and a new building had been commissioned.

Although the Liverpool Common Council had sought the talents of John Wood of Bath to create a new building, he had to decline their invitation due to pressure of existing work; instead he suggested that his son, known as John Wood the Younger, be offered the commission. Construction would take six years to complete, and although Master Wood did a splendid job in creating a stunning building for Liverpool, many of the Common Council would argue they ought to have waited for his father to become free to carry out the task. The new building was opened by the mayor, James Crosby, in a grand ceremony in 1754.

Although criticisms continued to rumble on for many years, no further alterations or additions were inflicted upon the Town Hall. Sadly, this beautiful building, a symbol of Liverpool's rising status, would be the victim of a severe fire on 18 January 1795 which gutted the building. Although parts of the building were saved, it would require extensive restoration work before the building could be used again. This disaster afforded the Common Council the excuse it required to commission another architect to create a new Town Hall. The Council appointed James Wyatt to create what would be Liverpool's fourth Town Hall. He carried out a splendid job, constructing a much larger dome, and added the distinctive Corinthian portico, at a total cost of £110,848. In 1811, the Town Hall was extended.

Although Liverpool's first newspaper, the *Liverpool Courant*, had been published as early as 1712, it had failed to catch on and soon faded away. The town's first truly successful newspaper, the *Liverpool Advertiser*, appeared 26 May 1756, published by Robert Williamson. Within a few years the paper had been bought out by Thomas Billinge, who changed the name to the *Liverpool Times*. Another newspaper arrived on the streets of Liverpool on 27 December, 1765, published by John Gore and called the *Liverpool Advertiser*. Both of these newspapers were published weekly and would hold the monopoly within Liverpool until well into the following century.

By the late-Georgian period Liverpool was a very well organised town, its population was still on the increase, and although matters

Liverpool's hinterland was once open countryside, occupied by grand houses and halls, homes of the gentry and the wealthiest merchants. This engraving depicts Roby Hall set in peaceful parkland. However, as Liverpool expanded it had an effect upon its hinterland, and today areas such as Roby and Huyton are home to massive housing estates. Author's collection

Liverpool's merchants built impressive terraced houses at Toxteth throughout the Georgian era. Examples of these houses still exist today: Rodney Street, Canning Street and Parliament Street are fine examples of this. And, No 62 Rodney Street, was the birthplace of William Ewart Gladstone on 29 December 1809, later prime minister on four separate occasions. The Author

were far from perfect, life for its inhabitants was improving, and significant progress had been made. In 1811 the Grammar School was closed and replaced by the North and South Liverpool Corporation Schools. The first gas lighting appeared in 1818 with creation of Liverpool Coal Gas Company, following the passing of an *Act of Parliament* in that year. The first building in the town to be lit by gaslight was the Town Hall later that year, and within the next few years gas lighting spread throughout the streets of Liverpool. The supply of gas increased with the founding of the Liverpool Oil Gas Works in 1823, and The New Coal Gas Company in 1834. It would be another forty-four years before electricity arrived.

4 ᴅᴇᴠᴇʟᴏᴘᴍᴇɴᴛ ᴏꜰ ᴛʜᴇ ᴘᴏʀᴛ

As Liverpool had originally been created as a naval port, simply to enable King John take his army across to Ireland, its continued development once this had been achieved was slow. For a period of just over five hundred years, Liverpool's port was fully controlled by the borough: initially by the burgesses, and later by the Common Council. Throughout this period, although the port was small, certainly compared to its neighbour, Chester, it did participate in some worthwhile trade, which brought revenue to the borough. Cargoes were purchased by the burgesses, and the goods distributed to the townspeople. By 1618, Chester's mayor had to begrudgingly admit that, although Liverpool's port was regarded as a dependant to that of Chester's, Liverpool had more vessels: Chester had fifteen, while Liverpool possessed twenty-four. The seventeenth century would have contrasting effects upon the port: increasing links with the Americas witnessed further imports arriving at Liverpool, including the arrival of the first shipments of tobacco; but the destructive years of the English Civil War would have a detrimental effect.

Liverpool, as a port, began to develop quickly following the ravaging years of the Civil War. The Lord Protector, Oliver Cromwell, recognised the role that Liverpool had played in the defeat of the Royalists on Marston Moor, and so granted the Port of Liverpool some independence in its own right, making it less subservient to Chester. Liverpool had lived through those years, with the constant harassment of neighbouring Chester, who regarded Liverpool as a mere creek. This difficulty continued to wrangle on. On many occasions Liverpool's burgesses had seized ships who refused to pay the appropriate taxes to their port, to the great annoyance of Chester.

Much greater significance was awarded to Liverpool in 1660, when the Surveyor General of Customs recognised Liverpool as being a port wholly independent from Chester, and that the port was now recognised on both sides of the River Mersey. Liverpool relished its new found independence, and imports boomed, with sugar and spices from the West Indies, and tobacco from the Americas. In a very short space of time, Liverpool could hold its own against other English ports such as Bristol and London.

However, in spite of such recognition, further expansion of maritime trade would be held back by the very geological properties that had made it a port in the first place. Liverpool's sea-inlet, the Pool, had provided the basis of a natural harbour. At around a thousand yards in length, it did provide a safe haven for the ships, though only at high tide: when this ebbed it left the boats stranded on the muddy sands. This was fine in the early days, when the vessels using the port were of such a size to be able to use this natural harbour, however, by the beginning of the eighteenth century, ships had increased in size dramatically, and so the Pool was no longer suitable: in severe weather they had no protection from either the winds or the waves. This inadequacy had been noticed in the later years of the seventeenth century and some ship owners had looked to construct their own makeshift harbour walls in an effort to protect their vulnerable vessels in bad weather. This had been frowned upon by the Common Council, and from the 1670s it became illegal to drop ballast into the Pool, with heavy fines levied for those carrying out such acts. Nevertheless, the inadequacies of the Pool remained and had to be addressed.

Around this time other ports had begun to improve rather than simply relying upon the natural protection: with wet docks being constructed at Bristol, Blackwell and Rotherhithe. For Liverpool to remedy this problem, it was proposed, in 1699, to deepen the Pool by dredging; though this was never carried out, for within a few years the concept of constructing a permanent dock had replaced it.

Liverpool's First Dock

The planned construction of Liverpool's first dock had been discussed for sometime, though never more so since the damage inflicted by the great gale of 1703, which had ruined many of the ships in the Mersey. The Liverpool Common Council began a campaign for a new dock, led by Sir Thomas Johnson, Liverpool's MP, and supported by leading merchant John Clayton. They consulted eminent engineers from the Port of London. George Sorogold, Britain's leading civil engineer, who had constructed the country's first dock, at Rotherhithe in 1700, was asked to survey the feasibility of this proposal. His findings were presented before Parliament in 1709, but faced strong opposition from the London merchants. Nevertheless Johnson was adamant that it should proceed, and won favour with many of his fellow MP's, and so the Bill finally received Royal Assent in the following year. However, Sorogold's commitments forced him to decline the offer to be its chief engineer. Johnson pleaded with him to change his mind: whether these pleas were successful or not were never known, as

Sorogold died soon after. This meant that the Common Council was left without a suitable eminent engineer to head the project.

By this time, Thomas Steers had gained a reputation for his engineering abilities in the south of England. Steers, born in Kent in 1672, had later joined the King's Own Regiment, and had been present at the Battle of The Boyne in 1690. He left the army seven years later, returning to his native Kent pursuing the engineering skills he picked up during his time in the armed forces. He married Henrietta Maria Barber, in 1699, they lived at Rotherhithe, and Thomas was employed as a junior engineer, working alongside Sorogold, during the construction of the Howland Great Dock. The Earl of Derby, who had commanded the Sixteenth Regiment, had met Steers previously, and now hearing of his engineering success, suggested him as an alternative to Sorogold. The Council accepted the Earl's suggestion, and Steers arrived in Liverpool in the May of 1710.

Steers was commissioned to construct the first wet-dock in Britain. He took complete control of the project, designing the dock and overseeing all aspects of the work, from excavation through to completion. Steers' plan was different to that proposed by Sorogold: he recommended draining the Pool and filling in around it. This first dock – thereafter referred to as the 'Old Dock' – was constructed by the implementation of huge gates at the lower end of the Pool, that allowed the access of vessels on the high tide, though they could be closed during the ebb, retaining the water. The Common Council granted the use of the land, and the sum of £500. The upper end of the Pool, which stretched as far as Whitechapel, was filled in.

The Old Dock was completed and opened to shipping in 1715, and was seen by all as a great triumph in the pursued enhancement of the port. And yet, shortly after the dock opened, it was forced to close for a period of six months or so, due to continued silting. Although remedied initially, the problem would continue to return to plague the Old Dock, and so Steers would continue to work on additional features and further improvements until 1721. The cost of construction ran far beyond the original estimates presented to Parliament in the Sorogold survey.

Steers also recommended that a dry dock now be added to Liverpool's waterfront, which meant a second Bill being placed before Parliament. This was successful, gaining Royal Assent in 1717, and construction began soon after. Steers built his dry dock, fed by the tide, just ahead of the Old Dock, followed by other graving docks, and the construction of the port's first Customs House. Although

Steers was elected to the Common Council and given the position of Dock Master in 1717, with an annual salary of £50, he was free to pursue his engineering career, which included his famous river navigations.

Liverpool's Second Dock, and increasing trade

The Old Dock suited the amount of shipping Liverpool was experiencing at that point in time; however, increasing demand soon outstripped its potential. To cope with this ever-increasing demand, Steers proposed the building of a new dock, in 1737, to handle the ever-increasing trade from the Cheshire 'wiches'. A Bill was completed and immediately placed before Parliament, which was readily accepted and received Royal Assent in the following year. Such was the need for this new dock that work commenced immediately. Although officially named the South Dock, it was more commonly known as Salthouse Dock, due to its immediate use by the salt trade. Compared to the Old Dock, the South Dock would be a huge leap forward for the Port of Liverpool: at 23,000 square yards it was almost three times as large as its neighbour.

This was to be Steers' final project, as he died in 1750, aged 78. The work on the South Dock would be completed by his assistant, a young unknown engineer from St Helens, Henry Berry. The work was completed on time, and the dock received its first cargo of salt in 1753. Berry had proved to be a most competent engineer, and a logical successor to the late Thomas Steers. Soon after, he was officially awarded the permanent position of Liverpool's chief engineer by the Common Council, and within two years would begin the task that would make him famous – the construction of the Sankey Canal.

The completion of this second dock made Liverpool Britain's premier port, eclipsing not only its earlier rival Bristol, but London too. By the mid-eighteenth century, Liverpool had advanced yet further, not only was it the country's largest port, it was rapidly becoming one of the most successful and important ports throughout Europe. The port had already benefited from political troubles within the continent: privateers had brought back much booty during the War of Austrian Succession, for instance. However, the single most important factor in the Port of Liverpool's development would be the importation of cotton for the Lancashire mill towns: the first cotton arrived in Liverpool in 1757, when almost 7,000 pounds was unloaded on the docks.

During the eighteenth century press gangs were common on the docks, seen as the only means possible of securing the appropriate number of seamen to man the men-of-war. Unsuspecting souls were made drunk and hoodwinked aboard; or cold conked in dark alleys, to awake the following morning on board ship. This practice was authorised by the authorities, who in the face of depleting numbers of seamen, knew harsh measures were needed.

However, during the Seven Years War, although the privateers had capitalised on the situation, their action would have serious repercussions: the blockade of the port by French ships for a period of weeks, and the eventual capture of several Liverpool vessels. During this period, privateers acquired so much wealth from the sale of captured foreign shipping that they gained influential status: this is born out by the fact that John Hutchinson, a former captain of a privateer vessel, was made Dock Master in 1759.

His appointment was an inspired choice and his work would assist the port in its continued development: including the calculation of the tides. As the ships using Liverpool's harbour increased, difficulties with the naturally occurring sand banks arose; vessels had to be careful on their approach to the mouth of the river, selecting the

Although Everton Beacon had been used as a guide to shipping for many years, as maritime trade at the Port of Liverpool increased, Hutchinson promoted the use of lighthouses, with the first being built at Formby and Hoylake in 1761. Author's collection

correct channel, otherwise they could easily run aground. Everton Beacon had been used as a guide to shipping for many years, but now something better was desperately needed. The early proposals of lighthouses were rejected by the Common Council, but the argument was finally won in their favour, and the first lighthouses were erected in 1761 at Formby and Hoylake. Hutchinson erected the Bidston Lighthouse in 1771.

More Trade, More Docks

By the late 1760s, Liverpool was home to around 260 vessels, and was in desperate need of more docks. George's Dock, Liverpool's third dock, was completed in 1771, designed and constructed by Liverpool's new dock engineer, Henry Berry; it measured 26,000 square yards. This dock, located at the bottom of Water Street, would serve the port well; in fact for many years it acted as the main dock. It was closed during the latter years of the nineteenth century, and filled in during 1900. Today, its former location is occupied by Liverpool's 'three graces': the Liver Building, the Mersey Docks & Harbour Board Building, and the Cunard Building.

The opening of the George's Dock ought to have begun a period of massive development, but in actual fact the port was about to enter

George's Dock, Parade and the New Baths, *by Samuel Austin, and engraved by Rob Wallis. Liverpool's third dock – George's Dock – located at the bottom of Water Street, was constructed in 1771 by Liverpool's second dock engineer, Henry Berry. It was so successful that it soon became Liverpool's main dock and would remain in use until the latter years of the nineteenth century. It was filled in during 1900, and within a few years the Liver Building, the first of Liverpool's famous graces, was built on the same site.* Author's collection

a period of decline. The American War of Independence inflicted a heavy blow to the Port of Liverpool, as it dealt extensively with the Americas: imports of tobacco and sugar were the bread and butter trade to the port, and the war denied them access to a huge proportion of their revenue. This led to great hardship within Liverpool, and such was the level of public feeling that there was civil unrest on the streets, which had to be quelled by the military. However, as devastating as this period undoubtedly was, once the war was over, by 1783, trade with America grew rapidly again.

A period of intense prosperity followed, which saw the waterfront change forever. In order to extend the capacity of the port, all the new docks would be built in the river itself. This was a massive undertaking, which involved the tipping of extensive amounts of hard-core. It was a worthwhile decision, however, and witnessed the opening of a host of new docks. Duke's Dock opened in 1773 for the Bridgewater deliveries, the King's Dock was the largest of Liverpool's docks when it opened in 1788, measuring 37,000 square yards, but it was surpassed by the Queen's Dock, when it opened in 1796, the first dock to pass 50,000 square yards (this would remain the port's largest dock until the opening of the Brunswick Dock in 1836, which surpassed 60,000 square yards). In the years following the War of Independence there were around 200 Liverpool ships, yet by the end of the century that figure had expanded, beyond all recognition, to around 1000. The increasing trade with the United States led to the construction of a huge tobacco warehouse alongside King's Dock in 1795.

Liverpool and the African Slave Trade

The reign of the House of Hanover had seen great changes to the Port of Liverpool. The *Treaty of Utrecht*, in 1713, opened up trade with the rest of the western world; in particular the Spanish granted Britain the right to supply slaves to her American colonies. This Slave Trade was recognised by the Government, with the appropriate passing of an *Act of Parliament*. The first slave ship had departed Liverpool for the west coast of Africa in 1708, where it collected just fifteen slaves and transported them through to the West Indies. In the early days, slave trading was seen as a most respectable business, and many high ranking individuals were eager to participate. For example, Foster Cunliffe, Mayor of Liverpool on three separate occasions (1716, 1729 and 1735), was actively involved in the slave trade.

At the start of the English slave trade, the ports of London and Bristol had the monopoly, but within a few years, Bristol was taking the lead over London. In 1730, following an *Act of Parliament* that supported the expansion of the Slave Trade, Liverpool began to take a much larger role in the proceedings. Just fifteen vessels sailed for the African coast that year, yet within seven years that figure had reached more than thirty. Liverpool's thirst for success meant that by the middle of the century it had surpassed both its rivals and was the main slave port in Britain, with fifty-three slave ships now operating. Soon it was one of the largest of its type in Europe, handling sixty per cent of the English trade and fifty per cent of the European trade too.

It was a profitable triangle. Liverpool ships carried slaves from Africa to the plantations of the West Indies and America, where they were traded for profitable commodities such as sugar, tobacco, rum, cotton and this formed what was referred to at the time as the 'African Trade' which accounted for around twenty-five per cent of the revenue of the Port of Liverpool during the eighteenth century. The number of slave ships grew. By 1760 Liverpool had almost seventy slave ships, and yet, by the turn of the century that figure had expanded to more than one hundred.

In the beginning, many of the slaves came from the prisoners seized by rival tribes who were constantly at war with one and other. Their leaders knew that trading prisoners, who they would have otherwise slain, meant the barter of goods from the white slave men. Later, however, as supplies became more scarce, raiding parties were common, penetrating deeper into the country, raiding villages at night and seizing the inhabitants, including men, women and children: all except the old, who had no value. Healthy young slaves would fetch around £100.

Although the majority of the slave traders cared little for their cargo, there were the notable exceptions. Hugh Crow, a Liverpool slave ship owner, was noted as being a good and fair-minded master – he had but one eye, and was known by his nickname 'Mind your eye Crow'.

Slaves had no market whatsoever in Britain. In fact, Parliament passed legislation in 1772, stating that should a black slave set foot on British soil, he would immediately become a free man. Thereafter, transactions of slaves were carried out at sea, well away from the port itself.

The calls for the abolition of slavery began to grow, finding support amongst the Quakers and Methodists. By the 1770s, when Liverpool had more than one hundred slave ships, the campaign had reached a point where people previously unconcerned by the trade began to question its existence. By the turn of the century the campaign to abolish slavery was gaining widespread support. William Wilberforce and Granville Sharp led the national campaign. Within Liverpool, the main slave port in Britain, the likes of William Roscoe and William Rathbone campaigned vigorously.

William Roscoe, born in Liverpool in 1753, in a small cottage at Mount Pleasant (close to the site of the modern *Adelphi Hotel*), came from a humble background: his father was a tenant farmer, and as a young man William worked for Gore's publishers. Despite his humble beginnings, he gained a decent education, and as a young man wrote poetry and studied art and literature. In later life he amassed a small fortune working as an attorney, and through very wise business dealings and investments became an entrepreneur, later going into merchant banking. Although not a burgess, Roscoe was voted as Liverpool's MP. As a Whig politician, he was a reformer, campaigning for the abolition of the slave trade. He bought Allerton Hall, and retired there in 1795.

Despite the success of the campaign to abolish slavery within Liverpool, the largest of the slave ports, such was the trade and income from slavery that many were against such activities to curb it. Liverpool merchants petitioned the House of Lords, stating that should the slave trade be abolished, it would have a severe affect on the prosperity of the Port of Liverpool. There was great hostility between the two sides, and whenever they met violence occurred – especially when the abolitionists attempted, on several occasions, to convert the seamen themselves. Such was the bad feeling within Liverpool that Roscoe, the local MP, lost his parliamentary seat.

Nevertheless, the campaign gained support in Parliament, and Wilberforce and his associates achieved their goal: the last slave ship to leave Liverpool was the *Mary*, owned by perhaps the most fairest of slave ship captains, Hugh Crow, in 1807. And against all predictions, the end of the slave trade did not mean the end of Liverpool's success and prosperity as a major port, quite the contrary, in fact trade increased through the intervening years.

Liverpool publicly apologised for its slave-trading heritage on the *International Day of Remembrance of Slavery and its Abolition* in August 2001.

Liverpool and the effects of the Industrial Revolution

The loss of the very profitable slave trade might have brought about recession and led to the decline of the Port of Liverpool, had it not been for the arrival of the Industrial Revolution within Lancashire. This change, in the mass-production of goods, made the port of Liverpool great again. As Lancashire became the heartland of the cotton industry, Liverpool became the premier cotton port.

Raw cotton was imported from the Americas, and was stored in

Liverpool's giant warehouses before being despatched, by a combination of the Bridgewater Canal or Mersey & Irwell Navigation and packhorses, through to the Lancashire cotton mill towns, such as Blackburn, Burnley, Rochdale and of course, Manchester; the opening of the Leeds & Liverpool Canal would improve transportation to the mill towns considerably. When completed, the finished articles, spun and woven into textiles, were returned to Liverpool and exported all over the world.

Liverpool's maritime trade had been temporally interrupted by the Napoleonic Wars, when the port once again returned to its roots as a naval base. French prisoners were housed in the town. Following the bankruptcy of Sarah Clayton, a colliery owner who had become a victim of the downturn caused by the American War of Independence, Liverpool Tower had been placed on the market, and would be bought by Liverpool's Common Council, who used it to house prisoners during the Napoleonic Wars, and remained in use as a jail through to 1811. It remained empty again for the following eight years, before it was demolished and the materials sold off; the majority of these were purchased, for £200, by a local corn miller by the name of Barrow. Today, nothing remains of the Stanley's former residence.

Sugar, spices, rum, and coffee etc., were also imported into Liverpool's docks. Within this trade from the West Indies, Liverpool was not supreme, but ran a close second to London; where Liverpool did excel was the importation of tobacco. A much larger tobacco warehouse was built at King's Dock, in 1812, to cope with the increasing trade. However, Britain was once again at war with America, and Liverpool suffered the consequences of the loss of imports. New avenues opened in Europe three years later with the ending of the Napoleonic Wars.

During this time Liverpool became a manufacturing centre – matches, flour milling and sugar refining became the norm, employing many people. By far the most famous sugar refiner was Henry Tate. Born in Chorley, in 1819, he spent his early years working in a grocer's store before moving to Liverpool to work in the sugar refineries. It was here that he made his name and his fortune by inventing a machine that could produce sugar cubes.

Other trades in Liverpool included pottery. The printing of pottery, using transfers, was another lucrative business, with many manufacturers sending their completed wares to Liverpool – including Wedgwood. Bricks and other masonry were another growth industry in the town, using local clay. Earthenware from the neighbouring town of Prescot had been exported through the port for many years, and later china was imported here too. One of the largest potteries, and the last to operate in the town, was the Herculaneum Pottery, which occupied a riverside location, later the location of the dock of the same name. Lime kilns were a common sight in Liverpool too: Lime Street, famous for its railway station, was originally called Limekiln Lane. Sugar factories were another source of prosperity, there were more than half a dozen operating in the town. With such dusty occupations, the brewing industry had a captive trade, as in many industrial towns there were many breweries here.

Further Expansion of the Port

In 1800, the Port of Liverpool's supremacy can easily be judged when compared to London, its nearest rival. Liverpool had six docks: Old Dock, Salthouse Dock, George's Dock, Duke's Dock, King's Dock and Queen's Dock, which covered thirty-six acres. London had only one, Howland Dock, which had been built in 1696. Despite this massive advantage, Liverpool was not about to rest on its laurels, and throughout the following years further expansion occurred on the riverside: Manchester Dock was built in 1806; Duke's Dock was

Liverpool's docklands increased considerably following the appointment of Jesse Hartley in 1824 as the Chief Dock Engineer. The following three images of the Canning Dock show the changes through the years: the first two, dating from 1836 and 1880, respectively, show the New Customs House, which opened in 1839, built over the Old Dock, which was demolished after the Second World War. In the photographs, taken in 1880 and 2003 respectively, the Pumphouse can be seen in the right of the picture, designed and built in 1878 by G F Lyster to power the hoists and pulleys. Although it remained in use until the beginning of the twentieth century, it later stood derelict until it was restored along with the Albert Dock in 1986. Author's collection

increased in overall size in 1811, while its neighbour Queen's Dock went through a period of expansion, between 1810-16.

The *1811 Dock Act* enabled the construction of the Prince's Dock, which opened in 1821, at a cost of £461,059. It also brought about a more structured management of the Dock Committee, consisting of twenty-one members, whose finances were controlled separately from that of the Common Council. However, the Committee only gained complete control in 1825, following great work by William Brown and William Huskisson MP. These men had persuaded Parliament that a wholly independent committee made up of like-minded men, including merchants and ship owners, should run the docks, for they alone had its best interests at heart.

William Brown was a Liverpool burgess. Born in Ireland in 1784, he had travelled to America at the age of sixteen. While there, his father founded Brown Shipley & Co, which proved so successful that in 1809 they opened a branch in Liverpool which was run by William. With the company having links on both sides of the Atlantic, William Brown soon rose to be one of the Liverpool's maritime leaders. Brown had sought reform in the administration of the Liverpool Docks and once this had been achieved worked strenuously for its continued expansion. Between 1825-57, the new managers successfully constructed a further twenty-one docks

This new committee appointed Jesse Hartley as Chief Dock Engineer in 1824. This proved to be an inspired choice, as Hartley would be responsible for much of the face of the river front during the nineteenth century. His first decision was to close and fill in the Old Dock in 1827, and commission the construction of the New Customs House. The foundation stone was laid on 12 August 1828, but it would be eleven years before the building was completed, at a cost of £180,000.

The Salthouse Dock was Liverpool's second dock and although it was begun by Thomas Steers, he died before completion and the dock was finished by Liverpool's new dock engineer, Henry Berry. This photograph, looking towards the north west, also shows the rear of the Albert Dock, the Pumphouse, as well as the Three Graces.
Author's collection

William Brown Street is one of Liverpool's most well-known thoroughfares, home to the Walker Art Gallery and the Library. Originally called Shaw's Brow, but was renamed in honour of one of Liverpool's greatest maritime merchants and benefactors. William Brown had been born in Ireland, but had made his fortune in America before moving to Liverpool in 1809. Here he increased his wealth several times over, but was more than willing to donate huge sums for the good of the people, including the creation of a library. Author's collection

From the end of the eighteenth century onwards all of Liverpool's docks would be constructed in the River Mersey itself - a massive undertaking, and a huge engineering feat, which led to the transformation of Liverpool's waterfront. This aerial photograph clearly shows the immense size of the Alexandra Dock, along with its massive grain silos. Author's collection

Hartley replaced the Old Dock with a host of new ones. He built the Clarence Dock in 1830, and Waterloo Dock in 1834, to handle the ever-increasing traffic. Brunswick, Trafalgar and Victoria Docks opened in 1836, followed by Toxteth Dock and the completion of the New Customs House in 1839.

With such a vast expansion to the dockside, warehouses were built throughout the area to handle the increasing trade; however, emphasis was placed on size and productivity, not on safety: this changed with a massive fire in Formby Street in 1842, which gutted many warehouses at a massive cost. The following year the *Liverpool Warehouse Act* was passed, which ensured greater fire precautions.

By the late 1830s the Port of Liverpool was booming. To cope with the ever-increasing amount of goods being imported, a new dock and warehouse complex was needed and Liverpool's authorities had earmarked the figure of £1 million for this to be achieved. Hartley's answer was the proposed construction of the Albert Dock, located to the south of George's Dock and in front of the Salthouse Dock, and he submitted both plans and scale models for the authorities inspection during 1841. Construction work began on this huge complex of docks and warehouses two years later, and it was completed in 1846, at a cost of £770,000. The new dock complex was officially opened in a grand ceremony, involving around 10,000 guests, by Prince Albert on 30 July. The royal party had sailed through to Liverpool in the Royal Yacht *Fairy*, and as it entered the port was met with spontaneous and rapturously applause and cheers from the crowds that packed the quays.

More improvements followed. The floating landing stage, known as St George's Pier Head, was constructed in 1847, which allowed ships to dock no matter what the level of the tide, improving the passenger facilities considerably. Other docks, such as the Nelson, Stanley and Wellington were built in 1849, and were joined by the Huskisson Dock four years later.

Liverpool: The Gateway to the New World

Liverpool's connection with the Americas had come through trade in rum, sugar, tobacco, and slaves. However, by the mid-nineteenth century there would be a new connection: transatlantic crossings. The first of these was made in 1838, by the steamer the *Royal William*. Although this came last in the race against Brunel's *Great Western* and *Sirus* from the port of London, it did open a new chapter for Liverpool. For against all odds, Cunard secured the contract for transatlantic crossings from 1840. This trade, though in competition

Although Liverpool's ship, the Royal William, *had come last in the 1838 trans-Atlantic race, Cunard secured the contract for trans-Atlantic crossings two years later. This new venture would prove profitable for Liverpool throughout the remainder of the century and long into the next, and huge liners would become a common sight in the Mersey, and passenger would depart Liverpool for destinations around the world. These four images clearly demonstrate the activity on the landing stages.* Author's collection

with both Bristol and London, would continue to expand, and prove profitable for Liverpool throughout the remainder of the century and long into the next.

However, not all the passengers sailing to the USA were the upper classes: emigration by the poor to the New World had begun in the 1820s, and by the 1840s and 1850s it had become a flood. So concerned were the American authorities that they imposed legislation whereby all emigrants required a bond to enter the country.

The River Mersey: A United Port
From the time of the Restoration, the Port of Liverpool had been recognised as being both sides of the Mersey. However, it was only during the nineteenth century that the docks would truly expand to both sides of the river.

Looking across the river from Liverpool's waterfront the cranes of Cammell Laird could once clearly be seen. Originally founded in 1824 by William Laird, as the Birkenhead Iron Works, this company would become one of the most famous ship builders. The company prospered after gaining several contracts to construct ships, and changed its name Laird Brothers Ltd at the turn of the century, when William's sons ran the company. Cammell Laird, came about soon after with the amalgamation of Laird Brothers and a Sheffield-based company, Charles Cammell & Company. This company was responsible for building some of the greatest ships afloat, including two *Ark Royals*, and during the Second World War they built over one hundred fighting ships.

Further expansion of the Cheshire side of the river followed the creation of the Birkenhead Dock Company in 1847, with the opening of the Egerton Docks in the same year. A Royal Commission was formed to look into how the expansion of the Mersey could best be achieved, and their recommendation was that one single authority was needed to control all of the docks on both sides of the river. Despite objections from Liverpool City Council, the Dock Committee resigned in 1857, and the Mersey Docks & Harbour Board, with twenty-eight permanent members, was born. However, to achieve its goals the MD & HB would have to silence its greatest critic, Liverpool City Council, and this was achieved by paying them £1.5 million in compensation for the loss of revenue. This change proved an expensive, though with hindsight a wise decision, as by the end of the nineteenth century the new port of Liverpool was the largest in the country.

The new company set to work immediately to improve the facilities at the port. The famous Liverpool Bar had been an increasing problem through the centuries, especially as the vessels using the Mersey increased in size. Ships were often delayed entering the port, having to wait for the tide to lift them across the bar. Towards the end of the century, the MD & HB employed dredgers to remove significant amounts of sand, increasing the clearance from five feet, to twenty-five feet. Stone embankments were constructed to prevent the sand seeping back, and lighthouses and buoys directed the shipping along the channel.

More docks were now required to cope with the ever-increasing level of trade. The MD & HB's first dock was the Canada Dock, which opened in 1859. In the following year the Great Float was added to the Cheshire side of the river – the largest dock on the Mersey, it handled trade with India and Pakistan.

Jesse Hartley, the man that had completely transformed Liverpool's waterfront, retired in 1860, and in the following year George Fosbery Lyster took on the role of chief dock engineer, a position he would retain through to the close of the century. Lyster's early years would prove to be a baptism of fire. Liverpool was still the main cotton port and vital to the Lancashire textile trade. It came as a devastating blow, therefore, when in 1861 the American Civil War began. The blockade of the Confederate southern ports on the orders of President Lincoln meant that Britain was deprived of raw cotton, which resulted in the Cotton Famine, as hundreds of mill workers were laid off. This brought massive deprivation to the cotton mill

RIVER MERSEY, LIVERPOOL. 219692

Liverpool Docks would become a prime target for the Luftwaffe during World War Two as it played its part in the Battle of the Atlantic, and throughout the conflict massive damage was caused to the area of the docks, many ships were sunk, and many lives were lost. These two pictures from 1939 show the port on the eve of war.
Author's collection

towns of Lancashire, with starvation a reality, the now unemployed mill workers had to rely upon charity, which established soup kitchens, to survive; the picture was equally grim in Liverpool. Although new avenues of supply were sought by the Liverpool ships, in India and the Far East, the famine continued to the end of the conflict. Once the trade links had been restored, raw cotton flowed into Liverpool and things returned rapidly to normality.

LIVERPOOL LANDING STAGE. 20970.J.V.

The Manchester Ship Canal

Throughout the Industrial Revolution, Liverpool had supplied Lancashire's textile industry with raw cotton, and exported its finished garments. It was the life-blood to the economic success of Lancashire, and in particular, Manchester. However, the Manchester merchants resented that they had to pay duties to the Port of Liverpool, and for a great many years, had talked of creating a direct link to the sea from Manchester. The Bridgewater Canal, although a vital artery, could only handle small cargoes, and what was required was a ship canal that could by-pass Liverpool completely.

The prospect of a ship canal by-passing the Port of Liverpool annoyed and concerned the MD & HB. Once the Bill was finalised Liverpool actively sought to prevent its passage through Parliament. However, although objections were submitted and upheld by Parliament, ultimately the Bill received the Royal Assent in 1885.

Thomas Andrew Walker became the chief engineer, and work proceeded at a reasonable pace until his death on 25 November 1889. Thereafter, the project was plagued with problems which delayed its completion. The Manchester Ship Canal was completed in December 1893, and was officially opened in a grand ceremony on New Year's Day, 1894, with the first voyage along the entire length of the completed waterway. The new waterway aroused great attention from the Victorian press, and on 21 May of the following year, Her Majesty Queen Victoria witnessed this engineering marvel at first hand, when she boarded the admiralty yacht *Enchantress* to travel the length of the Ship Canal.

Although the Manchester Ship Canal had initially been seen as a threat to the commerce of the Port of Liverpool, in reality it made little or no difference to maritime trade. The new century witnessed further expansion with the opening of the Gladstone Dock – built to take any size of vessel, at any stage of the tide – in 1913, by King George V.

The definitive image of Liverpool, the Three Graces, as seen from the River Mersey: a scene that's launched thousands of ships. Liverpool's classic waterfront is famous around the world, and has been nominated for the status of a World Heritage Site. Author's collection

5 | $\mathcal{T}$HE AGE OF LOCOMOTIVES

Although tramways had been used within the collieries for many years, and the Stockton & Darlington Railway had opened in 1825 in the North East, the construction and completion of the Liverpool & Manchester Railway is still regarded as the dawn of the age of locomotives. Even before completion, other towns were already calling for other lines to be built. Within a few short years the railway network, although still in its infancy, began to emerge – railway mania had begun, as businessmen raced to invest in this new, faster and more reliable transport medium.

The concept of creating a railway network had been suggested by several individuals through the years, though *Observations on a General Iron Railway*, written and published by Thomas Gray in 1820, had set the agenda. For although Gray's vision of towns and cities linked by rail had been ridiculed by many, his suggestion of linking Liverpool and Manchester found favour. The transportation of cotton between Liverpool's docks and Manchester's warehouses and cotton mills was vital to both towns economic success – so any new form of transport, especially if it were much faster than the canals, had to be worthy of consideration. Gray's brother, Charles, had business connections with many of Manchester's merchants and he helped to convince them that the proposal had a sound footing. However, although the Manchester men were interested, the driving force behind the project would be a Liverpool gentlemen: Joseph Sandars who was very enthusiastic about the railway and formed a committee in 1821, containing twenty-three investors, gathered from both towns.

Surveying the Line

Another interested party was the Birmingham entrepreneur, William James. He found the concept of railways fascinating and while on business within South Lancashire had travelled to Liverpool to seek out Sandars; the two men found they shared a common bond in the railways. James offered to carry out the survey, and Sandars agreed to fund it. However, despite James's enthusiasm, he was soon out of his depth, and the survey had to be abandoned. Undeterred, James visited the Stockton & Darlington Railway, where he discussed the matter of a railway linking Liverpool and Manchester, with a little-known engineer by the name of George Stephenson.

The following year, William James, together with his two sons, William and George, and George Stephenson's son, Robert, began another survey of the Liverpool & Manchester line, once again financed by Sandars. In reality, however, this was little more than a route finding exercise, not a survey in the true sense of the word, and achieved little more than James had done alone. Nevertheless, their actions were met with great hostility from the locals encountered en route – stone throwing was common, particularly around the industrial town of St Helens, and the surveyors came under attack. It was a difficult time for all, leading to massive delays, and the survey would take months to complete. Sandars, meanwhile, continued to spread the word of the intended railway, drumming up support amongst merchants in the region.

James never completed his survey. He fell ill (probably due to stress) and this delayed the project considerably. If this was not bad enough, soon after he found himself in court, sued by his brother-in-law. James' luck had run out, he was found guilty and jailed.

Early in 1824, Sandars published a pamphlet bestowing the benefits that the new railway would bring to the region. But this was nothing more than propaganda, for without a survey, the project was in crisis. In May the committee agreed that they ought to visit Stephenson and ask him to carry out another survey. Stephenson realised the publicity that such a project would create and agreed to carry out a new survey, arriving in Liverpool on 12 June. Just when the project looked doomed to failure, things began to turn around, when Liverpool's Common Council pledged their support.

Stephenson proposed that the railway should depart Liverpool from the north in order to avoid the gradient to the west of the town, and proceed through Fazakerley, Croxteth, Knowsley, St Helens, Leigh, Eccles and terminate at Salford. And yet this survey received even more hostility than either of the previous two, with opposition at every stage from landowners, canal proprietors, and the hostile public, who had been terrified by rumours that locomotives would cause fires, scare cattle, and make horses redundant. More reasoned objections came from the earls of Derby and Sefton, who were deeply opposed to the close proximity of the line to their respective estates, and Robert Haldene Bradshaw, head of the Bridgewater Canal Company, who denied Stephenson access to the Bridgewater estate.

With all of this to contend with, it is perhaps understandable that his survey was rushed. Nevertheless, Stephenson presented his findings to the committee, and the Bill received its first reading in the House of Commons on 8 February 1825, and its second reading on 28 February. Huskisson, President of the Board of Trade (and MP for Liverpool from the following year), made a passionate speech in the

The opening of the Liverpool & Manchester Railway became infamous for the death of the Liverpool MP and President of the Board of Trade, William Huskisson, who was knocked down by the Rocket at Parkside on the outskirts of Newton-le-Willows. A most regrettable incident, made more poignant for the fact that Huskisson had championed the cause of the railway. This engraving of William Huskisson MP, President of the Board of Trade, by J Cochran, originates from a painting by John Gladstone, done just three months prior to Huskisson's death. Author's collection

House in favour of the Bill. General Issac Gascoyne, Liverpool MP since 1796, also spoke favourably.

The seriousness of the matter meant that it had to be put before a parliamentary committee, which sat from 21 March. Expert witnesses were called from both sides; Francis Giles, an eminent canal engineer, was called by the opposition. The committee heard evidence from George Stephenson himself on 25 April. All went well on the first day, with Stephenson making many valid points regarding the need for an alternative form of transport to canals, however, matters deteriorated over the next two days, with his survey coming under close scrutiny: which was judged to have been rushed, and many of the calculations – for the height of the bridges, embankments, viaducts – were hopelessly inadequate. Stephenson himself was an easy target: an uneducated and inarticulate man, with a broad North-East accent – the opposition soon made him appear slow and backward. The Bill was rejected on 1 June, and Stephenson was dismissed soon after.

A New Beginning

Undeterred, the Committee, which by now had begun calling itself the Liverpool & Manchester Railway Company, approached the Rennie brothers, John and George, sons of the famous canal builder, and on 1 July they agreed to come on board. They were the logical choice, recognised nationally for their abilities as engineers, they were far more experienced at getting a Bill through Parliament than their predecessor. For the actual 'hands-on' work of the survey, they appointed Charles Blacker Vignoles, who began work immediately.

The surprising thing is, despite the hostility experienced in the previous three surveys, Vignoles experienced far less resistance from the landowners and canal companies. He even managed to successfully defuse the objections from the two earls, simply by bringing the line further south and far enough away from their estates. A revised Bill was presented before Parliament in February 1826. This time, with hardly any objections, the vote in the Commons was passed with 88 votes to 41, and the Bill gained Royal Assent on 5 May.

The Liverpool & Manchester Railway Company offered the Rennie brothers the position as chief engineers. Though, despite his failure to pass the original Bill, George Stephenson was still a firm favourite with Sandars. And yet the mere suggestion that Stephenson would be connected with the project angered the Rennies, who flatly refused to work with him; their best compromise being that Stephenson could consult on the locomotives, but not on the line itself. The Committee, now less than happy with the Rennies, were appalled to hear that the brothers were so busy with other projects that should they become the chief engineers, it was unlikely that they could afford to spend more than six days a year on the project, and rapidly came to the conclusion that the Rennies were no longer suitable candidates for the post!

Later that month, the Committee signed Josiah Jessop as the new chief engineer, with George Stephenson retained as his assistant. However, it was abundantly clear for all to see that these two engineers could not work together in complete harmony – whether this was a clash of personalities it is hard to judge – but it is reasonable to assume that the directors must have felt great unease as to how this would affect the construction. In the end, a possible crisis was averted by the untimely demise of Jessop immediately prior to work commencing, and as a result, Stephenson was made chief engineer in his own right on 3 July. To assist him, he brought in Joseph Locke, John Dixon, William Allcard and Thomas Gooch. Charles Vignoles, who was still connected to the project despite the Rennies' departure, worked through to February 1827, before resigning to work on other projects, including the Wigan Branch Line and the St Helens & Runcorn Gap Railway.

A Massive Feat of Engineering

There was a vast amount of work to be done. As the Liverpool Common Council had expressly forbade the railway from crossing any town centre streets, three tunnels were needed to reach Liverpool. Several embankments were required to maintain a level of the line within acceptable limits – including one at Roby, crossing the Ditton Valley, which would be over one mile long. And no less than fifty bridges had to be built, taking the line either under or over the turnpikes. Apart from this, there were some massive engineering feats to be overcome. The Olive Mount cutting would mean the extraction of half a million cubic yards of stone. Tunnelling and cutting was difficult and hazardous work, the rock was so hard in places that black powder blasting was used before the more conventional work, with pick and shovel was carried out. It was important that this was completed on time, so Stephenson placed Joseph Locke in charge. The Wapping Tunnel, another massive undertaking, would eventually be spanned by the famous Moorish Arch, designed and built by John Foster.

The crossing of the Sankey Valley, on the outskirts of Newton, was yet another headache. To achieve this Stephenson and Thomas Gooch designed a huge viaduct to cross both the canal and the brook, with nine arches sixty feet high in order to offer clearance to the masts of the Mersey Flats, whose construction was supervised by William Allcard. The St Helens Canal Company objected to the planned construction, fearing it would cause delays to traffic on their canal, and compensation had to be paid: the sum of £500 was paid in advance, and payments of £30 per day. The total cost of the viaduct, along with embankments built either side to raise the level of the line to the height of the viaduct, came to £45,000.

Of all the obstacles in the path of the railway, Chat Moss, a notorious mere, was the most formidable. Stephenson had placed Vignoles in charge of this section, supported by John Dixon; following Vignoles departure in February 1827, Dixon resumed total responsibility. It was an inhospitable place, which Dixon had discovered at first hand, when he slipped off a plank on his first day and sunk up to his waist in the bog! Crossing Chat Moss was going to be the project's biggest test.

More than 200 men were employed, constructing huge drains to

OLIVE MOUNT TUNNEL, NEAR LIVERPOOL

Construction of the Liverpool & Manchester Railway was a massive undertaking. The Olive Mount cutting and tunnel, seen in this first image, would involve the extraction of half a million cubic yards of stone, which had to be removed by blackpowder blasting as well as the laborious use of pick and shovel. Further along the route the crossing of the Sankey Valley would involve the construction of a huge nine arch viaduct. Author's collection

remove much of the surface water. So bad was the moss that the workmen wore boards strapped to their feet to prevent them from sinking. Once the excess water had been successfully drained, tons of hard-core were dumped on to the peat, in an attempt to construct an embankment; but this vanished without trace. Undeterred, the process was repeated, and continued until eventually it began to hold. More hardcore was added until it formed a stable platform on which to lay the track. However, despite the success of this method, it was not suitable throughout the moss: in some of the worse sections, where the bog was really wet, the engineers had to employ a much more radical method. First they dug out a channel and lined it with bundles of turf and heather, then they laid large, thick wicker mats on top to prevent the line from sinking. It was a radical – and some thought ridiculous – idea, but it worked! The track was laid, using fish-bellied type rails, on timber sleepers.

Crossing Chat Moss was finally achieved on New Year's day 1830, and, apart from costing around £30,000, it had also cost George Stephenson his reputation. The time it had taken to complete this section had caused Parliament grave concern, and in 1828 they had commissioned Thomas Telford to review Stephenson's actions. His findings – stating that 'progress was slow and disorganised' – encouraged rumours of Stephenson's imminent dismissal. Whether Parliament would have seriously considered replacing Stephenson at such a late stage is far from certain, but the question was resolved with the timely return of his son, Robert, who had been working abroad; thereafter things really began to come together for the railway.

A Question of Locomotives

With the railway's completion, attention turned to the movement of goods along it. Although the use of horse-drawn carriages had long-since been abandoned, an alternative method was still being considered. From the outset, George Stephenson had championed the use of steam locomotives, which he had installed on the Stockton & Darlington Railway, and to him were the obvious choice. Others, however, disagreed. The suggestion that wagons and carriages could be hauled along the line using a cable and a stationary engine had been proposed from one quarter, but soon rejected. The use of steam locomotives seemed the only answer, but the sceptics needed to be convinced: Stephenson invited a deputation to accompany him to the Stockton & Darlington Railway to witness his locomotives in action. The Stephensons put on such an impressive show for the

Rainhill is proud of its railway heritage. For it was here, in October 1829, on a stretch of track between Rainhill and Lea Green, that the age of locomotives really began, when Stephenson's Rocket out-performed its rivals. Rainhill Station was opened some years later and is famous for its 'skew bridge' which was built in line with the turnpike and not at right angles to the railway line! Author's collection

Committee that it was decided there and then to use locomotives on their railway.

Trials were organised at Rainhill, between the 6 -14 October 1829. The locomotives would be rigorously tested for speed, momentum, and reliability, with a prize of £500 to be awarded to the designer of the winning locomotive. Although there were five competitors, only four of them were locomotives. The *Rocket*, designed and built by George and Robert Stephenson at their Newcastle works; the *Sans Pareil*, by Timothy Hackworth of Darlington; the *Novelty*, by John Braithwaite and John Ericsson of London; the *Perseverence*, from Timothy Burstalls of Edinburgh; and finally, the fifth competitor was the *Cyclopede*, from T S Brandreth of Liverpool. The latter – which was not a locomotive, but powered by a horse – did not take part in the trials; however, it did travel along the line and entertained the gathering crowd.

Although the *Perseverence* was lightest of the locomotives, weighing less than three tons, it proved to be the slowest and was soon withdrawn. The *Sans Pareil* faired a little better, recording an average of twelve miles per hour, but suffered mechanical problems and was also withdrawn. Braithwaite and Ericsson's *Novelty* proved to be the fastest of all the locomotives, recording speeds of twenty-eight miles per hour, and might have won had it not suffered mechanical problems on the final day. Stephenson's *Rocket*, although slightly slower than the *Novelty*, recording speeds of almost twenty miles per hour, had proved the most reliable, passing all the tests with relative ease and, as the only locomotive still running, had come out top.

The Opening of the Liverpool & Manchester Railway

The official opening took place on 15 September, 1830, though the reception at either end of the line could not have been more different. Huge crowds had gathered at Edge Hill on the outskirts of Liverpool to witness the spectacle. The mood was upbeat, speeches were made and the crowd listened intently, while marvelling at the array of locomotives. The dignitaries – which included the Duke of Wellington, Sir Robert Peel, William Huskisson MP, Lord Wilton and Fanny Kemble (a twenty-year-old actress who had delighted audiences at Liverpool's Theatre Royal early that year), boarded the carriages hauled by no less than seven of Stephenson's locomotives. George Stephenson drove the *Northumbria*; Robert Stephenson the *Phoenix*; George's brother the *North Star*; Thomas Gooch the *Dart* and Joseph Locke had the

A rare image of Liverpool's first railway station - Crown Street - in the early 1830s; and *(below) Liverpool Lime Street Station today. Although Crown Street Station opened in 1831, it was far from satisfactory: it had to be reached via the tunnels cut through the natural sandstone, along which was such a steep gradient that the locomotives had to be hauled through by a cable attached to a stationary engine located at the Moorish Arch. The situation was far from satisfactory and Crown Street Station would be succeeded by Lime Street Station, with its huge arch glass roof that covered all eleven platforms, designed by George Stephenson, in 1836.* Author's collection

Rocket; the final two were the *Arrow* and the *Meteor*. And when it was time for the party to depart, signalled by the firing of a shot at just after 10.30 am, the crowds cheered and waved. However, the massive crowd that awaited their arrival at Liverpool Road Station in Manchester were far from jubilant, for unlike their Liverpool counterparts, they had a grievance: Manchester was the home of the radicals, who called for political reform and still vividly recalled the Peterloo Massacre that had occurred just eleven years earlier. The crowd here were hostile, they shouted abuse at the Duke of Wellington, and hurled stones. The party decided wisely to depart Manchester very swiftly indeed. The people of Manchester might well have despised the Duke of Wellington, but the people of Liverpool had take him to their hearts, and a column, some 118 feet high, bearing his statue, was erected at the top of William Brown Street, in his honour.

The First Railway Casualty

The opening of the Liverpool & Manchester Railway became infamous for the death of the Liverpool MP and President of the Board of Trade, William Huskisson. A most regrettable incident, made more poignant for the fact that Huskisson had championed the cause of the railway. His needless death could have been avoided had the passengers adhered to the instructions they had been given at the start of their journey: safety had been of paramount importance to the directors of the line, and to ensure that the passengers reached Manchester safely, they had instructed everyone to remain in the carriages at all times.

The journey had gone well until they stopped at Parkside, on the outskirts of Newton-le-Willows, to take on water. As the locomotives came to a standstill, rather than remaining inside the carriages, people became to disembark – perhaps to stretch their legs – and soon a large group had gathered on the tracks. Panic ensued when a whistle sounded, signalling the speedy return of the *Rocket*, on the Liverpool bound track: as the group ran back to the carriages, in the confusion Huskisson slipped and fell and was struck by the locomotive, breaking his leg. Although he was attended too, initially by Lord Wilton at the scene, and later by a surgeon at the vicarage at Eccles, the wound was so serious that amputation was deemed the only course of action. Sadly, despite the doctor's best efforts, Huskisson would die from his injuries later that evening. Years later a monument was erected at the scene, to commemorate the accident, which remains there to present day.

The arrival of the railways transformed the appearance of Liverpool: Lime Street had previously been a quiet, almost rural lane, but the creation of the railway station changed that forever. The railways led to the building of Liverpool's first hotels: **North Western Hotel,** *designed by Alfred Waterhouse, was once Liverpool's largest, boasting no less than 300 rooms, when it opened on Lime Street on 1 March, 1871. It closed in 1933, and, although there have been countless rumours of its demolition, it still survives today, as an overspill from John Moores University student accommodation. This picture shows the hotel in the 1920s.* **The Adelphi,** *Liverpool's most famous hotel, was built by the Midland Railway Company in 1868-9. It was rebuilt in 1901, though the hotel we see today stems from structural alterations which occurred in 1912, inspired by architect Frank Atkinson.* Author's collection

The Liverpool & Manchester Railway in Operation

The Liverpool & Manchester Railway was an immediate success, transporting not just freight, but passengers too. The railway had revolutionised travel, and reduced the journey time from days to hours. Nevertheless, there was much work still to be done. Although Manchester had its own station, Liverpool did not. Although work was completed on Liverpool's first railway station – Crown Street – early in 1831, it was far from satisfactory: the station had to be reached via the tunnels cut through the natural sandstone, along which was a steep gradient; so steep that the locomotives had to be hauled through by a cable attached to a stationary engine located at the Moorish Arch – although on the return journey, the slope acted in their favour and the locomotives descended by gravity alone.

Clearly Liverpool required a new station. A Bill was put before Parliament later that year extending the line from Edge Hill through to Lime Street, which would involve the digging of a tunnel almost a mile in length. Although Liverpool's Common Council threw a spanner in the works by refusing to let locomotives be used, and insisting they be hauled between Edge Hill and Lime Street, the Bill received Royal Assent on 23 May 1832. Lime Street Station, with its huge arch glass roof that covered all eleven platforms, was designed by George Stephenson, and although it was opened in 1836, work would not be fully completed for another three years. The current station dates from a rebuild in 1879, when for the first time, locomotives were finally allowed to enter.

Expansion of the Network

Stephenson, Locke, Dixon and Allcard remained with the Liverpool & Manchester Railway Company, supervising maintenance and line improvements, until 1833, before leaving to work on new projects: the success of the Liverpool & Manchester Railway inspired the creation of other lines, and more work for the pioneering railway engineers. The Grand Junction Railway received an *Act of Parliament* on 6 May 1833 to construct a line between Liverpool and Birmingham. William Allcard was chosen as one of the engineers on this important project, and construction went to plan, with the line opening to traffic in July 1837. In the following year Liverpool had a connection to London, using the London-Birmingham Railway. In 1839 rival companies – Chester & Crewe Railway, and Birkenhead & Chester Railway proposed linking Liverpool with the south, via a new line that would cross the Mersey at Fiddlers Ferry. However, despite their enthusiasm, this plan was rejected, and by 1840 both of these companies had been taken over by the Grand Junction Railway, who five years later would also take over the Liverpool & Manchester Railway.

Services between Liverpool, the Wirral and North Wales commenced in 1840, with the construction of the Chester & Birkenhead line. Although a proposal to link Liverpool with Southport and Preston was rejected in 1846, a rival plan linking Liverpool with Ormskirk and Preston was accepted. In the following year, a proposal to build a coastal line through to Southport, with stations at Crosby and Formby, received Royal Assent. And yet, although construction began in the spring of 1848, financial difficulties delayed completion until 1850. This line proved popular indeed and made Southport one of the most successful of the Victorian seaside resorts.

During the 1840s a number of lines were proposed to challenge the monopoly of the Liverpool & Manchester Railway, though not all were successful. In 1844, for instance, a line called the Bolton, Wigan & Liverpool Railway was proposed, and a Bill was placed before Parliament in the same year. However, a rival bid already before Parliament, to construct a line between Bolton and Bury, led to a merger and the redrafting of the Bill under a new heading of the Liverpool & Bury Railway, which was granted its *Act of Parliament* on 31 July, 1845. Departing Liverpool from the north, the new railway took a direct route, passing through Kirkby, Rainford, Wigan and on to Bolton and Bury. However, inspite of construction work being completed rapidly, and the new railway opening on 20 November 1848, this railway had been taken over by the Leeds & Manchester Railway Company on 22 July 1846, which became the Lancashire & Yorkshire Railway Company in July of the following year.

Further lines followed. In 1864, a line between Liverpool and Speke opened, utilising a section of the old St Helens Railway which fed the Garston Docks. In the same year, three more lines opened: the Cheshire Lines Committee formed and began operating services between Manchester, Chester and Liverpool, and Manchester, Warrington and Liverpool; and the Liverpool Central Station and Underground Railway received an *Act of Parliament* on 29 July, with services between Liverpool and the Wirral. However, construction of Central Station was unavoidably delayed, and only opened on 1 March, 1874.

Liverpool's Overhead Railway

Often referred to as the 'Dockers Umbrella', the Liverpool Overhead Railway was once one of the most famous landmarks in the city. The original concept had been first proposed in 1852, by John Grantham, but had been firmly rejected. Four years later, and the Mersey Docks & Harbour Board reviewed the option, but once more decided to reject. Nothing was mentioned of the proposal until 1877, when the MD & HB dusted off the plans. On this occasion, though the board was enthusiastic, the proposed railway would be rejected on the grounds of cost.

The opening of the world's first elevated railway in New York in 1870 excited the Liverpool dock engineer, George Fosbery Lyster, so much that he sent his son over to America to investigate the matter further. After evaluating all the facts, Lister submitted a favourable report to his superiors at the MD & HB, in which he stated that there was now a clear need for such a railway to be built in Liverpool. The MD & HB agreed, and planned a single line to operate steam locomotives. Despite the project proceeding so far, it would once again be shelved – this time following objections from a most unusual quarter Lyster who objected to the use of a single line, and the planned use of steam locomotives. Without his backing the plan was withdrawn.

In the meantime, Lyster was undeterred and worked on the plans in secret before submitting a new report in 1882. This time he proposed that the line ought to be much longer than the original plan: he now suggested that it should start at Herculaneum Dock and proceed through to Alexandra Dock. Although the Board were enthusiastic, lack of funds meant that the plans would need to be suspended for five years. Only in 1887 was a Bill put before Parliament; it passed without objection, and a new company was formed to construct and operate the railway, with Sir William Bower Forwood as chairman. A 999 year lease was signed 1 January, 1888, and the new company sought and received an *Act of Incorporation*, in the following July. Sir Douglas Fox and J H Greenhead were appointed as the consultant engineers to the project, with Francis Fox and S Cotterall employed as resident engineers, and work commenced 1 January, 1890.

The line was built quickly, working in separate sections that were eventually linked together. The Overhead Railway opened on 7 January 1893 and, through the years would become a very popular and wholly unique service in the area, that attracted a great deal of interest from visitors to the city. The line was extended and Riverside Station opened in 1895.

Often referred to as the 'Dockers Umbrella', the Liverpool Overhead Railway opened on 7 January 1893. It was used as much as a means to view Liverpool's impressive array of docks, as it was used as a means of transportation, and was advertised as offering 'a splendid view of the Docks and River'. Its eventual closure and demolition in 1957 shocked and upset many, sad to witness the passing of one of Liverpool's most famous landmarks. These photographs, taken during the 1930s, shows the elevated railway in better days. Author's collection

However, by the 1930s the line was already in a poor state, though it would linger on through the 1950s. Many had called for its closure, though equally as many had called for it to be saved. The final decision came in December 1956 with the passing through Parliament of a Bill proposing its closure and demolition. Work began demolishing the structure in the following September – crowds gathered to watch the famous Pier Head Station coming down in the November – and within twelve months it had all been taken away. Services along the riverside were replaced by a regular bus service.

Improvements to Public Transport

By the start of the nineteenth century many organised stagecoach operators had begun to operate. Bartholomew Bretherton of Liverpool began a stagecoach business in 1800, to destinations like Manchester and London, and local services to Warrington and St Helens. The first stage stop after departing Liverpool was Rainhill, where he built stables, large enough to hold 200 horses. However, soon after the completion of the Liverpool & Manchester Railway, Bretherton retired to Rainhill Hall, realising that this new form of transport spelt the end to his coaching business.

Despite Bretherton's foreboding, the railways did not mean the end of stage coaching. Peter Greenall, started a daily service, between St Helens and Liverpool, called the 'Regulator' in 1827. The passing of the *Municipal Act* of 1838, meant that the newly elected councils were now responsible for road construction and maintenance – which improved the road network considerably and by the middle of the nineteenth century even more coach operators had arrived on the scene.

The Liverpool Road and Railway Omnibus Company, owned by brothers William and Daniel Busby, had benefited with the arrival of the railways: in August 1848 they were contracted by the Southport Railway to carry passengers between Waterloo Station and Liverpool. Despite the termination of this contract just two years later, the company prospered opening new services. By 1860 they were operating daily services between St Helens and Liverpool; yet such was the level of demand that within a couple of years they had increased their service to three or four trips per day.

Public transport within the towns was still in its infancy. Omnibuses had been operating on Liverpool's streets since 1830. Though in reality these were little more than stagecoaches, still only operating on particular routes, carrying passengers from A to B, and refused to stop in between; only following the *Stage Coach Act* of 1832, did schedule stops at intervals begin.

Street railways had been pioneered in Birkenhead in the late summer of 1860, by George Francis Train. Proving a success, Train sought permission from Liverpool Council to operate such a service on this side of the river. However, he was not alone in this desire, for the Liverpool & Railway Omnibus Company Limited had also placed a bid. In the end the Busby brothers were successful, and would lay track along the length of the Liverpool-Prescot turnpike.

Horse-drawn trams were first established on Liverpool's streets in 1866, with the founding of the Liverpool Tramways Company. They laid their first tramline on Castle Street in that year, and soon spread to the other main streets. Following the passing of the *Tramway Act* of 1870 the company sought and gained the necessary permission to extend their network to the outskirts of Liverpool: the Dingle and Walton were the first to receive the service, followed by Aigburth in 1871. However, facing stiff opposition from other tramways, the Liverpool Road and Railway Company Limited, merged with their rivals in 1876, forming the Liverpool United Tramways and Omnibus Company.

In 1879, the passing of the *Use of Mechanical Power on Tramways Act*,

Liverpool's tramways were electrified in 1902 by the Atherton Brothers of Prescot. Trams came in a variety of shapes and sizes and became a common and popular sight on Liverpool's busy streets. Author's collection

led many towns – especially those with hilly routes – to invest in a fleet of steam-powered trams. Although Liverpool was reluctant to invest in these new machines, a trial was scheduled at Aigburth in the November, where an engine built in co-operation between the Liverpool Tramways Company and a local traction engineer called Duncan, was to put through its paces. The test attracted a vast crowd, including many dignitaries. The new engine – now powerful enough

to handle steep inclines, and haul even the larger carriages – sufficiently impressed the authorities that a further test was arranged, whereby the engine would be employed on the Liverpool Tramways circuit for the period of one week, in order to assess its overall ability. However, in spite of these tests, where the engine excelled, no further action was taken; even following further trials at Walton in 1881, steam-powered trams would never be employed on Liverpool's streets. Improvements to Liverpool's trams did arrive in 1902, when the Atherton Brothers of Prescot took over the network and introduced electric trams.

Trams were once a familiar sight on Liverpool's streets - these two pictures show trams on William Brown Street and Lime Street - and were popular with the travelling public. It would appear that they are set to make a welcome return in 2007, as Liverpool is to gain a metro tram system similar to that seen in other northern cities, such as Manchester and Sheffield. Author's collection

6   *T*HE BLACK SPOT ON THE MERSEY

At the start of Queen Victoria's reign Liverpool was a place of great contradiction. It had such a high level of violence and crime that it was referred to as *The Black Spot on the Mersey.* Yet, in stark contrast, the success of the port had merchants referring to Liverpool as the *Gateway to the West.* Throughout the Victorian era, however, Liverpool would be transformed from a humble town into a thriving industrial city; and from a minor port into a major one. However, before such heights could be reached, both Liverpool and its inhabitants would need to endure a period of great change.

A Growth in Population

Liverpool's population at the beginning of the eighteenth century stood at around 35,000. By 1800, the population had more than doubled, reaching almost 75,000. But the greatest increase would occur during the middle of the century: by 1851 Liverpool's population had boomed to a staggering 375,000. This upward trend would continue; just before the turn of the twentieth century the figure in Liverpool was estimated to be approaching 685,000.

Although Liverpool had long had an Irish population, this swelled to alarming proportions following the Potato Famine in Ireland. It is thought that of the 300,000 Irish that arrived at Liverpool, on their journey in search of a new life in America, around 60,000 chose to remain in Liverpool. The 1851 census confirms that the Irish community, close to 85,000, accounts for almost one fifth of Liverpool's population.

These new immigrants did not enjoy good times in Britain. Within Liverpool, as with the rest of the county, they were forced to live in the worst housing, the worst areas, and take the most menial, degrading jobs. Overcrowding was a massive problem. Such a huge and sudden rise in the town's population meant that the housing stock simply could not cope, and people crowded into any property that they could: at times as many as fifty people could now be living in one dwelling.

Of course, the Irish were not the only arrivals. Liverpool was by then a busy international port and had a mix of people from very differing origins, and throughout the century would build to become a multicultural town: including a large proportion of blacks, from the Negro slaves, together with Chinese, Welsh, and many Scots too.

Liverpool's Victorian streets were also filled with children: vagabonds, which survived through theft (images of Dicken's Fagin and his infant pickpockets immediately spring to mind!). Liverpool's Police Force made great efforts to remove these children from the streets and out of the taverns and brothels. The state played its role too, with the passing of various *Acts of Parliament,* and later, the introduction of state education helped to resolve the problem.

Strikes and public demonstrations were another difficulty for the police to handle. Within the early years of the nineteenth century, many trade unions were founded as a voice for the humble workers: in 1848 the Liverpool Trades Guardian Association was founded, consisting of fourteen trade unions from a variety of trades. Although the association would show solidarity with other workers – in 1854 they provided financial supporter to the striking Preston spinners – but their first major strike occurred in Liverpool in 1889, called by seamen protesting about their poor wages.

Immigration was another problem for the fledgling police force: Liverpool was a mixing pot of many different races and cultures, which sometimes led to friction – the mass arrival of the Irish, especially following the Potato Famine in 1845, caused some resentment amongst the population. Chief Constable Whitty retired in that year and was succeeded by Maurice Dowling, who held the post for seven years, when he was in turn succeeded by John Grieg who oversaw the force through to the 1880s.

However, despite all of these problems, Liverpool's Police officers carried out their tasks, and continued to make great strides in establishing forming of law and order. Although Liverpool has always had its fair share of crime, by the end of the century the police had ensured that it was no-longer a lawless town.

Poverty

Poverty was common in Liverpool; it had been rife during the previous century as Liverpool became an industrial port, but it became more acute during Victorian times. During the 1830s, such was the deprivation of children living in Liverpool that their death rate, from new born to reaching their third birthday, was around fifty per cent. By the end of the century matters had not improved: although the national child death rate was 142 per 1000, Liverpool's was 183, and the most deprived areas were even higher, Vauxhall, for instance was 264 per 1000. Those children who were lucky enough to survive faced a hard life. This could be spent on the streets: children,

Children gather around the Steble Fountain, outside the Walker Art Gallery in the early years of the twentieth century. The fountain had been a donation to the people of Liverpool by Colonel Steble, the former mayor, and had been erected in 1879. Although these children look respectable, Victorian Liverpool had been filled with vagabond children, bare foot and dressed in rags, that loitered on street corners and outside pubs, often thieving to earn a living. Author's collection

barefoot, stealing, selling what they could, or simply begging, were a common sight on Liverpool's Victorian streets. Ragamuffin children were everywhere: selling newspapers, doing odd jobs where they could find them, or just loitering outside public houses (or inside if they were fortunate), selling what they could.

For the most unfortunate, those that could no longer manage, then there was the dreaded workhouse. This was seen as the last resort by most of the poor, and yet Liverpool's new workhouse, built on Brownlow Hill in 1842, even though it had a capacity of almost 2,000 inmates, it was often filled to overflowing. Life within the workhouse

The Education Act of 1870 made the right of education open to all members of society, regardless of wealth or class. Further education was enhanced with the founding of University College of Liverpool in 1882, by William Rathbone, and the opening of the Technical School a few years later. Author's collection

was harsh, clearly designed to deter the poor from becoming a burden on society.

Pawnshops were a common sight on the old streets of Liverpool – the phrase 'one on every corner' related as much to pawnshops as public houses. People would hock whatever they could, from clothes to furniture, in order to make ends meet. As well as pawnshops there were moneylenders, who would provide loans, though at exceptional rates: any pauper going in debt to a moneylender – for what might seem a tiny amount – might well spend the rest of their days paying it off. For those that were working, and had some disposable income, the bookies might provide the temptation of gaining more: before the days of legal betting, bookie runners were common, stood on streets corners taking bets in clandestine fashion.

There was mass unemployment within Liverpool, far greatest than in the other parts of the region or the country. These were mainly amongst the unskilled workers, who had to look for basic labouring work. In late Victorian Liverpool there were becoming increasingly fewer jobs for the truly illiterate, unskilled workers such as these. As Liverpool began to expand, attracting new industries, efforts were made to educate the people. *The Education Act* of 1870 made the right of education open to all members of society, regardless of wealth or class, and education was enhanced with the founding of University College of Liverpool in 1882, by William Rathbone.

Public Health

Public health was not the great concern of the day in early Victorian Liverpool. Disease, as far as they were concerned, was a fact of life; the poor suffered from it, the wealthy did their utmost to avoid it. A severe outbreak of smallpox in 1830, had a devastating effect within the overcrowded industrial towns of Lancashire – accounting for almost 1,000 deaths in Liverpool alone.

Cholera was another killer of the age: between 1830 and 1870, there were four massive, and devastating outbreaks of the disease in England. Liverpool, as a major port, and a poor and overcrowded town, was a prime source of the disease, and it reaped what it sowed. A massive outbreak occurred during April 1832, which spread throughout the county, bringing death to towns such as St Helens, Wigan, Warrington and Manchester. And yet, despite being responsible for this chain reaction, Liverpool's inhabitants suffered the worst, accounting for more than half the deaths within Lancashire.

Another outbreak came in 1849, which proved to be far, far worse

Although most people think of St John's Market as the modern concrete precinct that we see in Liverpool today, its origins date back to 1822. This rare drawing by Austin, which has been engraved by Kelsall, offers us an image of the interior of the market in 1836 - and as we can see, it was a pretty busy place! Author's collection

than the previous outbreak, nationally accounting for over 50,000 deaths. Although industrial Lancashire suffered around 8,000 fatalities – 5,000 of them occurred in Liverpool alone. The disease was at its highest during the long hot summer, hundreds died every week in Liverpool and practically nothing could be done to avert this crisis. Cholera returned again in 1854 and 1866. Although both of these outbreaks were serious, the people of Liverpool were less affected than during the previous outbreaks.

Other diseases struck during that difficult century. Typhoid and typhus fever inflicted misery on the population on several occasions. In 1837, for instance, over five hundred people died from the fever in Liverpool. A far more severe case came a decade later, which had been brought to the port as the Irish escaped the Potato Famine, when 21,000 people died in the town.

Liverpool suffered from poor housing and massive overcrowding, which meant that viruses spread easily throughout the population, with quite devastating effects. Such was the outcry regarding these public health issues that a Select Committee was set up by the Government to look into ways of rectifying the situation and avoiding such occurrences in the future. The *Select Committee on the Heath of Towns* had been founded in 1840, and would lead to the establishment of Liverpool's own Board of Health.

Sanitation was a problem within Liverpool. Sewers were virtually none existent during the first half of the nineteenth century, with waste being dumped into the gutters directly outside the houses. Privies were emptied only when full, and the raw contents then deposited directly into the River Mersey. Such an environment assisted in the common spread of disease. This, along with the massive overcrowding, meant that Liverpool was a very unhealthy place in which to live.

Lancashire, with its overcrowded industrial towns, was deemed as the most unhealthy county in Britain: regardless of serious outbreaks, common illnesses, such as diphtheria, whooping cough and tuberculosis were more prevalent here than anywhere else in the country. Liverpool's adult death rate was around 40 in every 1000 people – almost three times higher than the national average. And, although it had a high birth rate, more than half the babies born in Liverpool would not live to see their fifth birthday. Such was the spread of the disease in Liverpool, that ships, anchored in the harbour, were used as floating hospitals in times of crisis.

Although the attitude of the privileged classes was to ignore the problem, some individuals did seem to care enough about the spread of disease amongst the poor to do something about it. Kitty Wilkinson was one of several kind-hearted people that aided the poor in the times of the disease outbreaks: in 1832, when Liverpool was being ravaged by cholera, she opened her kitchen for the poor, feeding them and washing the clothes in an effort to reduce the spread of sickness; its said that within one week she had washed more than 2,000 items of clothing (following her example, the Council opened public washhouses). Kitty would go on to help to educate the orphans of the cholera outbreak, and is lovingly remembered in one of the stain glass windows of Liverpool's Anglican Cathedral.

The plight of the poor and the continual spread of disease was something that concerned Dr William Henry Duncan, who became a leading reformer against such overcrowding and endemic illness within the town. Having graduated from the University of Edinburgh, he opened his general practice in Rodney Street during 1829, and also worked as physician to the Liverpool Dispensaries, who administered medical treatment to the poor.

Duncan worked out of the Liverpool North Dispensary in Vauxhall Road, one of the poorest areas of the town at that time. He was in the thick of it when the first serious outbreak of cholera occurred in 1832, and soon realised that by far the greatest number of deaths came from the residents forced to live in the courtyards and cellars, linking the spread of disease to mass overcrowding, poor sanitation, and the close proximity of sewers and rotting garbage. To reduce infection, Duncan pioneered mass hospitalisation and quarantine as the only way of curing the people and controlling the spread of the diseases. He also promoted the whitewashing of property to attempt to clean the living area, thus reducing, if not eliminating the breeding of germs.

The passing of the *Liverpool Sanitary Act* of 1846 led to the call for a medical officer responsible for the health of the borough. Although Duncan was awarded the position, the Council, lacking the necessary finances, chose to employ his services on a part-time basis. Nevertheless, the early years of his appointment proved challenging as he had to cope with the typhus outbreak, which was compounded by the hordes of Irish descending upon Liverpool in wake of the Potato Famine in 1845.

Liverpool's first full-time Medical Officer was Dr Trench, appointed in 1866. Cholera returned in the same year, as if to give the new Chief Medical Officer a baptism of fire. Although public health was now a concern, it did not prevent the return of serious outbreaks of disease: cholera returned in 1893, and smallpox in 1903.

William Rathbone, pioneered the process of nursing for the sick, regardless of their income or status, when he founded district nursing. Later he founded the Liverpool Training School, for nurses, and the Home for Nurses. A philanthropist, he was also a member of the Liverpool Select Vestry, aiding the poor and homeless, and campaigned vigorously for the improvement of living standards of the poor. As a direct result of his tireless endeavours, the first Society for the Prevention of Cruelty to Children was founded in Liverpool, in 1883, working at all levels to reduce the hardship experienced by children; they opened a shelter for children walking the streets, somewhere to sleep in the warmth, and be fed. Rathbone would continue his good work for the poor of Liverpool through to his death in 1902.

Housing

Victorian Liverpool, like its neighbour Manchester, was filled with poor, inadequate houses. The poor crowded into courtyards, containing squalid back-to-back houses, with few windows, offering poor ventilation and hardly any daylight. Sanitation was confined to communal privies, one, maybe two, to a courtyard. Families crammed into one or two rooms – in the more extreme cases there

Liverpool was the premier port for industrial Lancashire. All sorts of commodities were bought and sold at the Exchange. The following three pictures offer very different images of Liverpool's Exchange: the first is a drawing by G Pyne, engraved by Thomas Dixon and dates from 1836, and two photographs, one from the late-nineteenth century, and the other from 1939. In the centre of all three images is the Nelson Memorial, erected in 1823 in honour of his victories over Napoleon. Author's collection

could be as many as twenty people sleeping on one floor. Despite Dr Currie's condemnation of the use of courts within Liverpool in 1801, at the start of the Victorian era there were almost 3,000 courtyards still in existence within the town. Within these slums it was estimated that there were close to 18,000 homes not fit for human habitation. It is thought that one in five of Liverpool's inhabitants lived in these circumstances. Even in 1840, its been estimated that there were around 20,000 people living in cellars. Cellar dwellings were being condemned and closed by the authorities, but it was a slow process; ironically, just as they were beginning to make some progress, the passing of the *Liverpool Improvement Act* of 1842 recognised a distinct shortage of housing, in light of the vast number of immigrants now arriving in the port, and the cellars were reopened again!

Another acute problem in Liverpool were the lodging houses. Being a

Liverpool was the principal port for the Lancashire textile industry. Although the Cotton Brokers' Association had been founded in 1841, and became the Liverpool Cotton Association by 1882, they traded at the Exchange, along with other commodities until Liverpool's designated Cotton Exchange opened in 1906. Author's collection

port, lodgings for sailors had always existed in the old streets that surrounded the Dock Road. However, these were some of the worst lodgings, a den of thieves and a hotbed of disease, and the landlords exploited the situation by charging excessively high rents. To combat this the Sailors' Home had been created in Canning Place behind the Customs House, funded by charitable donations, and Prince Albert laid the foundation stone during his visit to Liverpool in 1846.

Despite repeated calls for improved housing for the poor, little change came. Only by the 1870s did the pattern of house building start to change, by-laws were passed ruling such dwellings as unfit, and demolition began. Their replacements were terraced rows, with gardens or yards to the rear, containing individual privies. Outside water closets came in a little later. These terraced houses were divided from their neighbours by an alleyway: these, in Liverpool were particularly narrow and often winding, and were referred to locally as 'jiggers'. These sorts of houses and jiggers would become commonplace throughout Liverpool.

As for the managers and bosses, well understandably they lived in much better homes – terraced or semi-detached – built on the outskirts of the city, such as around Sefton Park, far enough away from the grime and pollution of the industrial centre. A little later, areas such as Roby and Huyton became the rural retreat for Liverpool's merchants and entrepreneurs. It is somewhat ironic that by the twentieth century both Roby and Huyton would become the over-spill for Liverpool's working classes, and noted for huge council house estates.

Water and Sanitation

For centuries, Liverpool's inhabitants had extracted water for cleaning and drinking from the River Mersey. This often proved to be unhealthy, for even though its waters were considerably cleaner in pre-Industrial Revolution days, its contents was not free from germs. Springs at Copperas Hill had been used, though sold to the inhabitants at often extorted rates. At the turn of eighteenth century water had been brought into Liverpool on wooden carts from Bootle and sold. In the later years, as Liverpool's population continued to expand, its water supply came from two different sources: the Bootle Water Company and the Liverpool & Harrington Water Company, who gained their supplies from deep sunk wells (the Bootle Company had 11 such wells, or bore holes and the Liverpool Company had but five wells, including those in Old Swan and Wavertree). However, supplies were erratic and the drinking water often substandard. Even by the Victorian era the quality of the water was wholly lacking, and complaints from residents and business alike flowed into the newly elected Liverpool Council.

Although water was on tap, the quantity of taps was minimal. The vast majority of courtyards – containing several families – would be serviced by a single tap. The water pressure and the continuation of supply was woefully inadequate: periods of no water supply were far more common than one might think. This erratic supply led to long queues for water: in the poorest areas queuing for water might take several hours.

A committee was formed in 1845 to investigate water supplies, and how they might be increased. It did not get very far, for two years later, the matter was still under investigation. Eventually, the committee concluded that the supply of water was wholly inadequate for the size of the population it had to serve; neither company was producing sufficient levels of water to cope with the need. The result was the passing of the *Liverpool Corporation Waterworks Act*, which gave the Council power of compulsory purchase, which would finally bring the entire supply of water for Liverpool under a single operator.

The committee's solution, to cope with the ever-increasing demands on water, were two fold: the expansion of the underground sandstone reservoirs, and the construction of artificial reservoirs at Rivington. The concept of the Rivington Scheme, as it became known, was the brainchild of the civil engineer, Thomas Hawksley. His proposals for the construction of the Rivington Reservoirs, and the underground pipeline from there through to Liverpool, caused much local debate.

There was massive opposition to this scheme, mainly on the grounds of both cost and time of construction. In fact such was the level of debate, both publicly and within the Council, that an enquiry was set-up, chaired by Robert Stephenson, son of the famous railway engineer. His investigation into the pro's and con's of the scheme was thorough, though with great disappointment to the anti-Rivington activists, Stephenson's report found in favour of the proposal. Work on construction of the five reservoirs and the aqueduct commenced in 1852, and would take a further five years to complete.

During the days of the eighteenth century, Liverpool's sewage was removed from the streets by men using a cart and ringing a bell to warn of the dangers to health. The first sewer system was laid in the early years of the following century, though the men with the cart and bell continued to operate until the 1840s in some parts of Liverpool.

The daily collections continued, and waste-dumps were created on the outskirts of the town where the waste was deposited. The early sewers were large, man-sized structures, that also took the rain water. They were not connected to any form of other water supply: this meant that the waste was not moved throughout the system (in fact, there was once legislation, designed to prevent the wastage of water, that forbade the connection of toilets to the water supply and sewers). It was only following the appointment of John Newlands, as the first Borough Engineer, in 1856, that the matter of working sewers was addressed. Over the next decade improved sewers were installed. Water closets began to appear in the 1870s, that had sufficient pressure to flush the waste along the system.

To improve public health the streets were paved, and gullies were installed to ensure the streets remained free from flooding and were cleaned regularly. Waste was cleared from the streets regularly by the Corporation, and burned in incinerators.

By the 1870s, Liverpool's growing need for increased water supply led to the suggestion of piping water from Ullswater and Haweswater in the Lake District, in a joint project with Manchester. Bateman, who was a consultant engineer, felt that it could supply around forty million gallons per day to both Liverpool and Manchester. However hostility between the two Councils eventually led to the plan falling through. Instead, Liverpool chose an alternative source for its growing need for water: Lake Bala in the mountains of North Wales.

Improvements in Local Government
The Reform Act of 1832 brought great changes to parliamentary representation, but the passing of the *Municipal Act*, three years later, brought greater powers to the people. For the first time town councils, such as Liverpool's, could be elected from the people, by the people, and not just fellow councillors, as had occurred on Liverpool's Common Council. William Brown was elected as one of the new councillors, and was also sworn in as an Alderman. The Borough of Liverpool expanded its boundaries under this new legislation, bringing areas such as West Derby, Toxteth, Everton, Kirkdale within its authority. The newly elected council had plenty of work to do. One of its primary concerns was the reform of housing and living standards of the people, and the demolition of the slums.

Greater status followed: the Incorporated Chamber of Commerce was founded in 1850, but what Liverpool really sought was city status. Manchester, their arch rival, acquired this accolade in 1853, but Liverpool was denied the privilege. The quest continued, and

Liverpool's fourth Town Hall was built by James Wyatt, who did a splendid job, constructing a much larger dome, and added the distinctive Corinthian Portico, as drawing of G Pyne, engraved by W Watkins, clearly shows; and it was equally beautiful internally as it was externally, as these three drawings by Harwood and engraved by R Winkles, offer a glimpse of the classic ballroom and news room. Author's collection

Liverpool had gained the right of an Assize Court in 1835 and St George's Hall had originally been the designated location for this institution. The photograph (below) is a rare image of Liverpool's County Sessions House. Author's collection

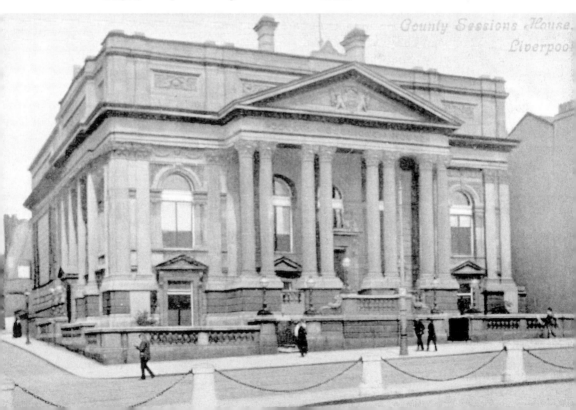

Liverpool finally gained city status in 1880, with the granting of a charter from Queen Victoria – twenty-seven years after its rival, Manchester. With this increasing status, Liverpool City Council applied for the right to elect a Lord Mayor, and this was granted in the charter of 1893. And two years later, the city's boundaries were further extended to include Wavertree, Walton; Garston was added in 1902, and Fazackerly two years later.

Leisure and Recreation

Despite such a gloomy picture of Victorian Liverpool, life did begin to improve. In the latter years of the nineteenth century, the Victorians suddenly started to take the plight of the working classes living within the industrial centres much more seriously than ever before. Great emphasis was placed on providing places for leisure and recreation, so the working classes might be able to escape – albeit temporally – the squalor and pollution.

For the people of Liverpool, they would attempt to escape the poverty of the town by trips to the seaside; this influx to the coast made the trips on the Liverpool ferries, by far the best way to cross the River Mersey, increasingly popular. Ferries crossed from the Pier Head through to Birkenhead, Seacombe and New Brighton. The main Liverpool Ferries left from the Princes Landing Stage, from the southern end (the northern section was used for steamers travelling further afield to the likes of Ireland and the Isle of Man). The Birkenhead Ferry, started in 1821, by George La French. By 1835, the Woodside, North Birkenhead, and Liverpool Steam Ferry Service Company had taken over the ferries. Though their control of the service was short lived, experiencing financial difficulties caused the service to become erratic; and in 1842 it was awarded to the control of the Birkenhead Corporation. In 1847, the St George's landing stages were built at Liverpool, used by the ferries and passenger liners. The first threat to the ferry service came with the construction of the Mersey Railway in 1886.

The seaside resort of New Brighton, was formed by a Liverpool builder by the name of James Atherton, in 1830, by purchasing 170 acres of sandhills on the Wirral Peninsula, from which he hoped to create a northern resort that would rival that of Sussex's Brighton. To raise the sufficient finances to form the original hotel, with a regular ferry service to bring his customers from Liverpool, he had to raise £12,000: this was done by advertising the benefits of this potential resort, so close to the open sea, with long sandy beaches and clear fresh air. Shares were sold at £100 and there were plenty of takers.

ARGE'S GARDENS, LIVERPOOL.

The need for open spaces, gardens and parks for the working classes was addressed in the latter years of the nineteenth century. These two photographs show St John's Gardens and Sefton Park. Author's collection

Trade experienced by the ferries increased during the latter part of the nineteenth century and the beginning of the next. The Wirral being the closest part of 'leafy Cheshire' to Liverpool soon meant that it became a desirable place to live; far enough from the industry and pollution of the city, and yet, with the ferries operating such a regular service, close enough to live for the managers of the companies there.

The rush for open spaces for the poor and working classes, led to the sudden creation of public parks, designed solely for recreation. Throughout the nation former estates were either donated to, or purchased by the town and city councils to create parks. The first of Liverpool's public parks was Princes Park, with land donated by Mr Yates; but this was soon followed by Wavertree Park and the Botanic Gardens. Sport came into its own too : the famous Grand National founded in 1837. One of the supporters of this great steeple chase was William Lynn, proprietor of the *Waterloo Hotel*, he leased a race course at Aintree. Lord Sefton was another avid supporter. The first *Adelphi Hotel* was built by the Midland Railway Company between 1868-9. Liverpool *Daily Post*, founded in 1855. The advent of railways to the coast led to the creation of seaside resorts, such as Southport and Blackpool, which were immensely popular throughout the Victorian era.

Liverpool's Victorian Architecture
In great contrast to the poverty and deprivation experienced by the majority of the people in Liverpool, during the nineteenth century, the same century saw the building of some of its finest buildings.

Certainly the most famous is St George's Hall, built in the Greek Revival style by the young architect, Harvey Lonsdale Elmes in 1854, on the site previously occupied by the Seaman's Hospital and the Liverpool Infirmary. Liverpool had gained the right of an Assizes Court in 1835 (previously held in Lancaster), so St George's Hall had been built and designed to hold such a court, however, prior to completion, it was decided that instead this building was to be used as an exhibition hall and concert arena.

The first public library in Liverpool opened in 1850, in Duke Street, following the forming of a library committee early that same year: this later became known as the Libraries & Museums, and later still, Libraries, Museums & Arts Committee. The first library was far too small to cope with the huge demand that was placed upon it, although a place to use the Royal Institution was proposed, it was later abandoned. William Brown donated the finances for the construction of a grand library, laying the foundation stone himself in

The Walker Art Gallery was founded by the industrialist and former mayor, Andrew Walker, in 1877, and it continues to play a significant role in the city today, providing many thousands of visitors each year a glimpse of one of the finest collections of paintings, sculpture and other works of art seen in Europe. Author's collection

Liverpool is blessed with some beautiful and classic Victorian architecture, though by far the most famous is surely St George's Hall, built in the Greek Revival style by the young architect, Harvey Lonsdale Elmes in 1854, on the site previously occupied by the Seaman's Hospital and the Liverpool Infirmary. Author's collection

1857. The building was completed three years later, designed by architects Thomas Allom and John Weightman. Sadly the building became a victim of an incendiary during an air raid in 1941 – although it required substantial rebuilding, the original façade was retained. The Municipal Buildings, built between 1860-66 became the work of two separate architects, for although construction was commenced by John Weightman, the work would be completed by E R Robson. The Walker Art Gallery was the inspiration of Andrew Walker, industrialist and former Liverpool mayor, who commissioned architect Vale in 1875. The building opened to the public two years later, though was enlarged by Cornelius Sherlock in 1882. Today it offers visitors a glimpse of one of the finest collections of paintings, sculpture and other affects seen in Europe. Next door stands the Picton Reference Library, designed by Sir James Picton, which opened in 1879.

A City Transformed
At the beginning of the Victorian era Liverpool was a violent, deprived place, full of poor housing and poverty. During Queen Victoria's reign Liverpool had witnessed a great many changes – the creation of the railways, the expansion of the port, the establishment of public health, running water and adequate sanitation, and an improvement in housing. Although there was still a great deal to be done, its fair to say that by the end of the century Liverpool was a cleaner and safer place in which to live, and could no-longer be described as the *Black Spot on the Mersey*.

7 𝒫OVERTY & WAR

The twentieth century dawned with little apparent change for the people of Liverpool. Life continued regardless, the problems they had experienced in the previous century followed them into the next: mass poverty, poor housing and low wages. If the inhabitants looked to a 'brave new world' from the twentieth century, they were to be disappointed. For although the new century would eventually deliver change, it would be achieved at the expense of those that lived through the first half of the century.

The City's Architecture
Many of Liverpool's best known buildings were erected during the early years of the twentieth century, and yet still dominate the city skyline today. Of Liverpool's many famous and instantly recognisable

These following three photographs offer us a picture of Liverpool in the first decade of the twentieth century, and proves it was a busier place then as it is now: St George's Crescent in 1900; Lord Street and North John Street in 1908. Author's collection

buildings, surely the 'Three Graces' are the most well-known.

The Liver Building, completed between 1908-11, and home to the The Royal Liver Friendly Society, dominates the appearance of the Pier Head, and has become the definitive landmark that people around the world associate with Liverpool. The Port of Liverpool Building of 1907, has also become a notable landmark on the waterfront, with its green dome; and with an inscription inside that reads: *They that go down to the sea in ships and do business in great waters; these see the works of the Lord, and his wonders in the deep.* The Cunard Building, a grand structure made of Portland stone, was built during the years of the First World War, as the headquarters of the premier passenger line.

And let us not forget Liverpool's two magnificent cathedrals: Liverpool's the city with a cathedral to spare. The construction of an Anglican cathedral had been planned since the end of the nineteenth century: when St John's church was demolished in 1898, the vacant location behind St George's Hall was initially thought the ideal position for the cathedral. However, on reflection, the planners felt that the presence of two colossal buildings side-by-side would be too over powering for the city centre. Other locations were considered, but in the end the grand position on St James Mount, overlooking both the city and the river, seemed the most fitting location. The Anglican Cathedral, Church of Christ, is the older of Liverpool's two cathedrals, and with its 466 foot high tower, it is visible for miles around. The architect was a twenty-one year old Catholic, Sir Giles Gilbert Scott, who originally had a vision of a cathedral with two tall towers. Work commenced in 1904, when Edward VII laid the foundation stone on 19 July, though it was only consecrated in 1924, by King George V.

Although the Roman Catholic Metropolitan Cathedral of Christ the King was actually scheduled for construction on Brownlow Hill, in 1928, it was not completed until 1962, and was consecrated five years later. Just as the Anglican Cathedral had been designed and built by a Catholic, it seemed only fitting that this Catholic Cathedral be created by an Anglican architect, Sir Frederick Gibberd. As with the Anglican Cathedral, the architect originally had a very different concept in mind: Gibberd had planned a structure with a huge dome, on the line's of Wren's St Paul's, but it never escaped the drawing board. The cathedral that was created was an almost futuristic design, that has become yet another striking feature on the Liverpool skyline and is affectionately known locally as Paddy's Wigwam or the Liverpool Funnel.

LIVER, CUNARD AND DOCK OFFICES, LIVERPOOL 221096

The early years of the twentieth century saw the construction of three buildings that would not just alter the aspect of Liverpool's waterfront, but become so famous that they would be thought of as the definitive image of the city the world over - they were of course the 'Three Graces': The Liver Building, built between 1908-11, for the Royal Liver Friendly Society, and home to the famous 'Liver Birds' positioned at either end of the building - often referred to as 'one watching the river, the other watching the football'. The Port of Liverpool Building, built in 1907, which bears the inscription: They that go down to the sea in ships and do business in great waters; these see the works of the Lord, and his wonders in the deep. *And the Cunard Building, built in Portland stone during the years of the First World War.*
Author's collection

LIVERPOOL CATHEDRAL. (14)

93365.J

Liverpool's Anglican Cathedral, situated on St James' Mount, with its 466 foot high tower, dominates the city's skyline and is visible for miles around. Designed by Catholic architect, Sir Giles Gilbert Scott, work commenced in 1904, when Edward VII laid the foundation stone, though it was only consecrated in 1924, by King George V. These three pictures offer very different aspects of this grand structure, during construction and completion. The intended location of the cathedral had proved difficult and for a time St John's Garden had been a possible contender.

Author's collection

The city's famous *Adelphi Hotel*, standing proudly on Lime Street, was originally built by the Midland Railway Company between 1868-9 – although the hotel was rebuild again during 1901. However, the *Adelphi Hotel* we know today stems from structural alterations which occurred in 1912, inspired by architect Frank Atkinson. Through the years many important guests have stayed here.

Civil Unrest

Although the new century brought further hardship for Liverpool's workforce, it also gave their employers notice that they would not stand idly by and take it. The first example of Liverpool's growing militancy occurred at the end of the first decade, with the Transport Strike of 1911. This started with ship owners refusing to employ anyone who was a member of a trade union. A clear show of solidarity was needed and a strike was called. This seemingly took the proprietors by surprise, hitting them hard and they soon caved in: agreeing to accept trade unionists, and raising pay accordingly.

However, rather than just accepting what was a clear victory, the Liverpool strikers vowed to remain out on strike until their claims were met in full. What's more, they actively sought to extend their industrial action, by calling on other transport unions to support them. Their rallying cry was heard and they were soon joined on strike by fellow trade unionists from the railways, trams etc. In no time at all the entire city was at a complete stand still.

The strikers called their first public meeting at Great Crosshall Street, on Friday, 11 August. Although the mood was upbeat, some minor rioting occurred. A further meeting was scheduled for the Sunday, and this time the venue was St George's Plateau. Massive crowds, estimated at around 25,000, turned up to hear Tom Mann, chairman of the Liverpool Strike Committee, give a rousing speech. Once again, the mood of the vast majority of the crowd was upbeat, however, on the fringes things were a little more heated. Some minor disturbances occurred in Lime Street and the police were called in, who it must be said acted harshly, attacking the tightly packed crowd with truncheons. Soon an all out fight between the strikers and the police ensued. The police summoned reinforcements, who charged the crowd with batons and the strikers responded by hurling bricks at the police. Hundreds were injured, the majority of which were taken to Liverpool Royal infirmary. Ever since, that eventful day has been referred to as Bloody Sunday, and is as well known in Liverpool, as the Peterloo Massacre in Manchester.

Three days of rioting continued in which several hundreds more were injured. And even further trouble occurred when those arrested at the meeting were taken before the magistrates on the following Monday and Tuesday. Missiles were thrown by the waiting crowds at the police and the vans containing the prisoners. The Eighteenth Hussars were called in. Some rioters attacked their horses and the order to open fire was given, which resulted in the death of the two rioters. The strike finally ended on 24 August.

It is perhaps easy for time to look scornfully on the actions of the Liverpool strikers. And yet many of the people who had attended the meetings – and even those that participated in the rioting – had done so for the best of reasons. Where they militants, or just workers looking to stand up for their rights? It is refreshing to realise that within a few short years, those same men would serve 'king and country' during the Great War, and many would never see Liverpool again. The irony is, that on the spot where the rioting of Bloody Sunday took place on St George's Plateau, now stands Liverpool Cenotaph, a permanent monument to those that gave their lives during the Great War.

The next episode of civil disorder came in 1919 with the Police Strike. Liverpool Police officers were some of the lowest paid in the county – their weekly wage was considerably less than the dockers. The role of the police in a hard city like Liverpool was demanding, and the men that attempted to maintain law and order on Liverpool's streets had simply had enough.

The plight of the poor within Liverpool is obvious, and so, when the strike was called, and the streets were no longer being patrolled, it was simply an opportunity too good to pass up. Wholesale looting of shops and premises occurred on the weekend of the August Bank Holiday, which coincided with the police strike. So intense was the level of looting within Liverpool that it was claimed in the press that not a single shop window remained intact in the whole of the city.

Eventually, the Police Strike ended when some of the less-committed officers returned to work, and life returned to normal. Although not all was well within Liverpool, the 900 or so police officers that had remained on strike were dismissed, and they were blacklisted throughout the borough.

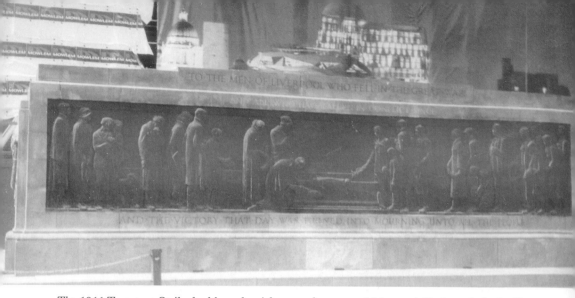

The 1911 Transport Strike had brought violence to the streets of Liverpool. Strikers clashed with police on Lime Street and William Brown Street and as things got out of hand much blood was shed. And yet, were the strikers as bad as they were portrayed - for within a few years many of those men would lose their lives fighting for 'king and country' in the Great War; and the Cenotaph would be erected close to the spot were the riot originated. Few could have imagined that within twenty years another world war would begin and account for many more lives. Author's collection

The Great War

On the eve of the Great War, calls for volunteers was led by the Earl of Derby, and wholly responded to by the men of Liverpool and its hinterland. Liverpool played a key role, as headquarters of the Western Approaches. During the war, although the fighting was far away, the Port of Liverpool was closed in fear of submarine attack, and many of Liverpool's fine ships failed to return to port again. The most famous of these is surely the sinking of the *Lusitania*, which was torpedoed by German U-boats on 7 May, 1915, just ten miles off the Irish coastline. Of the nearly 3,000 on board that day, almost half lost their lives as the ship sank within ten minutes of being struck. The news of this horrific incident circulated around the world; of all the horrors that occurred during the Great War, this alone seemed to capture the feelings of so many. This one act by the Germans changed the course of the war: over one hundred Americans lost their lives that day, which changed public opinion in the States to such a degree that they were now drawn into the conflict. Liverpool played host to the arrival of the American forces, commanded by General Pershing.

Later in the conflict, Liverpool became the main despatch area for troops, not just to France and Belgium, but further afield such as Turkey. Even the humble Mersey ferries were used in the conflict, transporting troops to France and Holland. And, on one famous occasion, took part in a mission to transport Royal Marine Commandos for an assault on the U-boat pens at Zeebrugge. It was as a result of this heroic work that the ferries, *Daffodil* and *Iris*, were award the title *Royal Iris* and *Royal Daffodil*, respectively.

The Great War took its toll on Liverpool. Although hostilities never came to the city directly, the people of Liverpool certainly went to the hostilities – and almost 14,000 of them lost their lives on a foreign field.

Post-War Liverpool: A land fit for heroes

The period immediately following the end of the Great War was far from pleasant, and certainly not 'a land fit for heroes'. It was the time of the Great Depression, when unemployment reigned, hardship and poverty were rife, and soup kitchens became a common sight on Liverpool streets, which continued into the following decade. And despite the working classes rejoicing at the creation of the first Labour Government in 1924, life did not improve. Indeed, matters went from bad to worse, and culminated in the General Strike just two years later.

In the years that followed, things began to pick up a little, with some prosperity returning. The Lancashire textile trade had reached its highest ever output, and the Port of Liverpool, the primary port for the importation of cotton, was booming, handling more than three million bales of cotton in that year. However, this new-found prosperity would be short-lived, never again would the Lancashire mills see such good times. Poverty and mass unemployment continued in Liverpool throughout the 1930s – often referred to as the Hungry Thirties – reaching double the national average by 1939.

Social Housing

The slum housing that existed in Liverpool and its suburbs during the nineteenth century had not been fully eradicated, far from it, much of the poorest housing still lagged way behind what they deemed as acceptable for human habitation: often as many as half a dozen families still had to share a single water tap. There was a great deal of work still to be done.

Matters were exacerbated by the fact that, in the years immediately following the Great War, the demand for new housing was even greater than before. However, the new houses that were under construction would be priced way beyond the budget of the working classes which forced them to remain within the slums. This intolerable situation caused great concern to the Government and inspired Dr Addison, the Health Minister, to pass the 1919 *Housing Act*. This made the local authorities solely responsible for the housing needs of their individual area, and so forced the councils to provide adequate housing to the poorest member of society. This was answered in two separate forms: by building what would later be referred to as council houses, or, by the councils subsidising a percentage of the private landlords excessively high rents, so that the poor could afford to live there. This was a quite radical step, and surely would have paved the way for the creation of the modern welfare state, had it not been for the fact that *Addison's Housing Act* was repealed soon after!

Liverpool's poor would have to wait another five years for the introduction of affordable housing, with the passing of the *Wheatley Housing Act* of 1924, which actually set aside the finances for the building of municipal housing in the most deprived areas. Many thousands of houses were erected under this legislation, that is, until it was terminated by Parliament, who deemed the council house policy as too expensive. Speaking in the House of Lords in 1928, Lord Melchett described the state of housing for the poor as being 'far superior than that that existed before...' and that it was now a 'relatively small problem'.

The 1930 *Slum Clearance Act* saw the demolition of the worst of slums – but this only fuelled the need for even more replacement housing. Within a couple of years the municipal building programme returned. With the 'standard family' consisting of a mother, father and two children (one boy and one girl) all municipal housing would now contain three bedrooms, if only to preserve decency. These new houses, built on a pattern of just twelve to the acre, cost £500 per house. This type of council house became common, not just in the suburbs of Liverpool, but throughout the region – and are still in use today.

Liverpool's population was still on the rise, and the growing need for more and more housing meant that the city would need to expand. With parliamentary approval, Liverpool City Council annexed Allerton, Childwall and Woolton in 1913, Croxteth and West Derby in 1928, followed by Speke four years later. And throughout much of the 1930s and 1940s, Liverpool would witness the construction of more than 30,000 new homes – a mixture of houses and flats.

The Story of Liverpool Airport

Liverpool gained its airport, on the outskirts of the city, at Speke in 1933. Work had been ongoing for the past eight years, which included draining and levelling the land at a cost of almost £40,000, but the new airport was officially opened on 1 July of that year, by the then Secretary of State for Air, Lord Londonderry. The original terminal was built in the popular art deco style of architecture by Arthur Landstein. Today, the Grade II listed building has become the *Marriott Hotel*.

Liverpool was an ideal location for a passenger airport, with such a large amount of traffic created by the port and in particular its transatlantic liners. Equally, trade between Liverpool and Ireland – Belfast and Dublin in particular – had increased. Although principally flights from the airport were through to Ireland, Blackpool and the Isle of Man, within a few years that had expanded with flights into Europe, as well as further destinations within the UK. Through the years the airport gained new routes and an increasing number of passengers – throughout the 1950s it was handling almost 100,000 per annum, resulting in the construction of a new runway in 1966, opened by Prince Philip.

Although throughout the intervening years Speke Airport competed against its regional rivals, by the 1980s the airport closed, and was replaced by a new airport, referred to as Liverpool Airport, owned by Peel Holdings. This has come along in leaps and bounds. Now the centre of Easy Jet's expanding empire, the airport is used by vast numbers of travellers throughout the year: in 1991 it was handling almost half a million passengers, but within five years that figure had increased to 620,00. Through the years Liverpool Airport's status has continued to increase, and it currently handles two million passengers per year. However, as air-travel continues to grow, Liverpool Airport would need to expand to stay abreast of competition from Manchester Airport and other rivals. With projected passenger numbers suggesting that Liverpool could be handling eight million passengers per year by 2030, rumours continue to circulate that a second runway might be added.

In 2001, it was announced that construction would begin on the new £32 million terminal due to open the following year, and that the airport was to change its name, to honour one of Liverpool's famous sons: The Liverpool John Lennon Airport, opened by Yoko Ono, with the slogan: *Above us only skies.*

Public Transport

The Liverpool tramways had been acquired by the Liverpool Corporation in 1897, who had pressed ahead with the electric trams, with the last of the horse-drawn trams being withdrawn in 1902. At that time the Liverpool United Tramways Company owned around 150 omnibuses. The electric cables necessary to run the new fleet of trams were laid by the James and Jacob Atherton of Huyton, proprietors of BICC in Prescot, who had operated a similar service in both Prescot and St Helens. The electric trams proved immensely popular within Liverpool. However, despite their popularity, competition was on the horizon.

In other towns electric trams were gradually being phased out by the late-1920s and replaced by trolley buses. Although Liverpool reviewed the concept of installing trolley buses on its streets, and the Corporation placed a Bill before Parliament for their operation, public opinion rejected their use. In fact, the only trolley buses seen in Liverpool would be those that travelled between the city and St Helens.

As early as 1907, Liverpool Corporation had considered the use of motor powered buses on the streets of the city, though a committee concluded that there was insufficient trade for such vehicles, and the plans were withdrawn. However, Liverpool would later be drawn into using motor buses by accident, when they purchased Wooltons motorised services in 1911. Such were their popularity that within three years, new bus routes were established around the city. During the Great War, with the movement of troops, civilian and freight, motor buses were employed to connect areas not on the existing tram routes.

However, the popularity of the electric trams within Liverpool meant that the Corporation was reluctant to allow motor buses to supersede them. And yet, it was only putting off the inevitable: the turning point, swinging the argument in favour of the motor bus was the constant need to repair and replace the existing tramlines throughout the city routes, due to excessive wear and tear. Buses were, in that case cheaper and far more economical to run than their tram counterparts. Gradually, buses were allowed to operate on some tram routes. Trams witnessed a reduction in services during the 1930s and 1940s, and they made their final journey in 1957.

Road Transport and the Golden Age of the Motor Car
Lancashire County Council took overall control of road improvements at the start of the twentieth century. New roads were planned to improve existing routes between towns and cities; it was during this period that the term 'main road' was first adopted. Although road planning was governed by the County Council, construction was controlled by the town/city surveyors.

The economic significance of Liverpool and Manchester over the region's prosperity meant that superior transport links between these two key cities was vital. The existing route along the A57 was wholly inadequate, winding through the narrow streets of Eccles, Warrington, Prescot and Huyton, before eventually reaching Liverpool, it often caused congestion.

Plans to alleviate this problem had begun as early as 1913, though the Great War had intervened. The 1920s saw a massive increase in motor traffic, which only added to the existing problem. The respective councils of Manchester, Liverpool, St Helens and Warrington proposed the construction of a new road, that would connect the cities of Liverpool and Manchester in one direct line. This was placed before Parliament and gained approval in 1926. With an estimated cost of around £2-3 million, it was a huge investment: this would be jointly funded between the Government, who funded two-thirds of the cost, with the reminder coming from the respective councils. From the outset, the new road was named the East Lancashire Road.

It was, for the time, quite an undertaking, equal to that pioneered with the building of the Liverpool-Manchester Railway a century

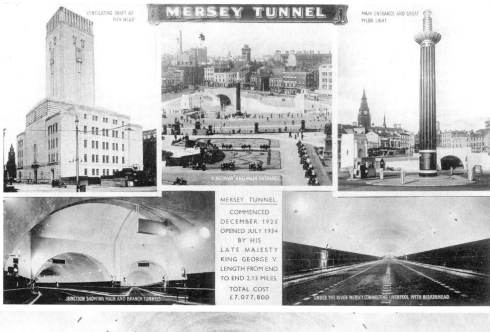

MERSEY TUNNEL

VENTILATING SHAFT AT PIER HEAD

'KINGSWAY' AND MAIN ENTRANCE

MAIN ENTRANCE AND GREAT PYLON LIGHT

MERSEY TUNNEL
COMMENCED
DECEMBER 1925
OPENED JULY 1934
BY HIS
LATE MAJESTY
KING GEORGE V.
LENGTH FROM END
TO END 2.13 MILES.
TOTAL COST
£7,077,800

JUNCTION SHOWING MAIN AND BRANCH TUNNELS

UNDER THE RIVER MERSEY CONNECTING LIVERPOOL WITH BIRKENHEAD

1863   Under the River Mersey Connecting Liverpool with Birkenhead

The day after opening the tunnel, the king opened the East Lancashire Road. Designed and constructed by John Brodie, Liverpool's chief engineer, this was a 'road of the future' specifically designed to connect the cities of Liverpool and Manchester in one direct route and relieve congestion. The Author

earlier. No other road of its size had been constructed in this country before: some twenty bridges would need to be erected throughout the distance. The road engineer given the task of carrying out this feat of engineering was John Brodie, Liverpool's chief engineer (who built Liverpool's first ring road – Queen's Drive – in the same decade). The road would be built in separate sections, and then joined together later; although overall administration was controlled by Lancashire County Council, each council would be responsible for the construction of its individual section.

On 18 July 1934, the Mersey Road Tunnel was opened by King George V. To construct this permanent link between Lancashire and Cheshire over one million tons of earth had to be excavated, and the work cost in the region of £8 Million. The ventilation shaft had been designed by architect H J Rowse in the style of classic monument of building, and is nothing like what you might expect a ventilation shaft to look like. Author's collection

Although construction was meant to commence in early 1929, objections from landowners affected by the road delayed the project for a few months. The first sod was finally cut, in an elaborate ceremony, on 29 April, by Sir John Aspell, chairman of the Highways Committee. The road, which was a modern design, made of concrete with a tarmac surface, proceeded on schedule and within the budget. And was officially opened on 19 July, 1934, by King George V.

This was not the only piece of modern infrastructure from which Liverpool benefited. The Mersey Road Tunnel (Queensway) was also completed in the summer of 1934, and opened by King George V on 18 July. Over one million tons of earth had to be excavated, and the work cost in the region of £8 million. Prior to its official opening to traffic, pedestrians were allowed to walk through the tunnel in 1933-4. Its completion was seen by many as a massive threat to the very existence of the Mersey ferries – and many thought they would never survive the completion – but, the ferries continued to attract passengers regardless. Liverpool's second road tunnel, the Wallasey Tunnel (Kingsway), opened in 1971.

Creating the National Game

The origins of Association Football, or soccer, began in the latter years of the nineteenth century, with the late-Victorian thirst for leisure and recreation. The Lancashire Football Association formed in 1878, consisting of amateur teams that had been formed primarily from the mill workers and miners. The early matches often lacked clear rules and self-discipline: the Victorians worked hard, and played hard! By the time the Liverpool & District Football Association was formed in 1882, things had moved on, and the game was becoming much more organised: with the new ruling that all clubs had to play matches on enclosed grounds, not in the park. As the game developed, the Football League would be created within four years.

Liverpool had four separate clubs: St Domingos, Liverpool Caledonians, and Liverpool Ramblers, and another club just up the road at Bootle. St Domingos football team had begun as a Sunday School activity, and developed into much more: changing their name to the Everton Football Club, and creating a much larger following. This investment was beneficial, with Everton enjoying the most success of the original four teams.

In 1882, Everton moved from Stanley Park to the *Sandon Hotel*, owned by a local entrepreneur John Houlding, who soon became the club's largest benefactor, investing considerable amounts of money to enable the purchase of professional players. However, Houlding's generosity came at a price, as he wanted the club run his way. He secured a new ground at Anfield Road, where much better facilities, both for players and spectators, were subsequently built.

All was going well until 1892, when Houlding announced that they should purchase this land and form a limited company to run the club on a professional basis. However, a disagreement amongst the club's board caused the plan to be rejected, and set in motion a series of events that would see the birth of Liverpool FC.

Everton FC broke its ties with Houlding, departing Anfield and constructed a new stadium at Goodison Park. Undeterred, Houlding remained at Anfield and formed his own club, Liverpool Football Club. However, having two clubs within Liverpool caused problems, not least of all that Liverpool FC were prevented from joining the Football League, and had to play their early matches within the Lancashire League instead.

The following season saw Liverpool join the Football League, and the intense rivalry between the two Merseyside teams began! Both teams prospered during the first half of the twentieth century; both won the FA Cup. Everton won the last championship, just before the Second World War brought such activities to a close.

The Second World War

The rise to power of the Nazi Party, and the subsequent re-militarization of Germany, caused instability and spread fear throughout Europe. As the crisis in Europe deepened, Britain knew that it would eventually be drawn into war and in spite of the appeasement offered by the Prime Minister, Neville Chamberlain, the country began making the necessary preparations.

The people of Liverpool were only too aware that once war was declared, their city would become a prime target for the Luftwaffe. The fear of air-raids resulted in the construction of communal shelters by the Corporation, and the people of Liverpool kept busy constructing Anderson shelters – named after their creator Sir John Anderson – in their back gardens. Thousands of gas masks arrived in the city in the autumn of 1938, ready to be distributed in the event of war. And Parliament passed the *Training Act,* which began being implemented in the summer of 1939 where young men were given compulsory training in weapons.

Confirmation of people's worst fear came on the morning of Sunday, 3 September, when in a radio broadcast on the BBC, Prime Minister, Neville Chamberlain, speaking from the Cabinet Room of 10 Downing Street, announced '… we are now at war with Germany'.

The people of Liverpool were only too aware that once war was declared, their city would become a prime target for the Luftwaffe. The following three pictures - the Town Hall, Water Street and Lord Street - date from 1938/9 when Liverpool was on the eve of war. The Author

TOWN HALL, LIVERPOOL.

2/7093 J.V.

Liverpool, as a major port for the Atlantic Convoys, delivering the much-needed supplies of food to the nation, ranked high on the targets of the Luftwaffe. As a prelude to invasion, the Germans knew that they must destroy Liverpool, as the director of the Western Approaches, it would be the co-ordinator for the Battle of the Atlantic: the nerve-centre was deep underground, below Derby House at Exchange Flags. Liverpool would play a key role in the Battle for the Atlantic, between 1939-43, as the premier port for vital imports from the USA.

The first bombs that fell on Liverpool came in July 1940, though the heaviest of the bombing came in the summer of the following year. The May of 1941 and the first two of weeks in June, referred to as the May Blitz, accounted for almost half the casualties in the city during the whole of the war. Bombing throughout this period was continuous, night after night the bombers reeked havoc over Liverpool: 79 bombing raids were carried out, destroying almost 10,000 homes, and damaging a further 120,000 homes. Throughout the duration of the bombing almost 4,000 people died in Liverpool (almost 1,500 in the May Blitz alone), but twice that number were seriously injured. Liverpool's dockland took a pounding, and massive amounts of damage was inflicted on the area: although the Albert Dock escaped damage, one of the victims was Hartley's Customs House in Canning Place, which was so badly damaged that it had to be demolished.

Not all the German air raids dropped bombs, incendiary devices were just as effective: St Luke's Church, at the top of Bold Street, designed by architect John Foster in 1811, became the victim of an incendiary on 10 May, its burnt out remains have been kept intact ever since to serve as a memorial to the bombing that Liverpool endured. The houses at the top of Bold Street had received massive damage a few days earlier. The total cost of the May Blitz came to almost £500,000.

Thankfully, the city's children had been evacuated; although there had been many tearful exchanges on Lime Street Station as the children were separated from their parents to begin the long journey to the safety of the Welsh countryside, it had been worth it in the long run.

For the civilian population life was very hard during the war years. The uncertainty of loved ones fighting somewhere abroad, the lack of news, mixed with the constant fear of air raids, made the thought of planning for the future seem unrealistic. Nevertheless, life had to continue: the housewives continued to go about their daily chores,

St Luke's Church, standing at the top Bold Street, was severely damaged by incendiaries during the Blitz and although only its shell remains, it stands as a permanent reminder of the death and destruction that was inflicted on Liverpool by the Luftwaffe during the Second World War. The Author

and shop the best they could, despite the endless queues and the rationing. The government inspired the motto *Dig for Victory*, in an effort to persuade people to grow their own produce on small allotments. The dark winter nights were made longer and darker than ever before, as the clocks were put back two hours instead of the normal one, and the blackout was compulsory, enforced by law and the ARP patrols. Street and road signs disappeared, the names of railway stations followed suit – getting around, even for the locals, was often difficult. There were countless drives for vital resources – rubber drives, paper drives etc., and all the iron railings disappeared from around the parks, schools and public buildings, taken to be melted down for the war effort. Endless fund raising occurred – often to purchase 'a Spitfire for the RAF' – which helped to keep morale high. People had to be on their guard, don't talk to strangers, always remembering that 'careless talk costs lives'.

The attack on Pearl Harbour in 1941 brought the Americans into the war. For many of the GI's, their first glimpse of Britain was disembarking at Liverpool Docks in 1942, prior to being transported to their new home at Burtonwood, near Warrington. The arrival of the Yanks caused mixed feelings from the locals; while many of the ladies greeted them seemingly with open arms, many of the local lads were less than pleased. For a nation that had been on the ration for more than three years, it must have been quite an insult to have to accommodate the Yanks that seemingly had everything! Fights in the pubs and dance halls around the city became common place – and this resentment led to the saying, 'overpaid, over sexed and over here'.

It was a great relief when, on 8 May 1945, the end of the war in Europe was announced over the radio: throughout the country, people danced in the streets. And with the hostilities finally at an end, the lights came on again all across Liverpool and the other towns and cities in the country. However, although the conflict within Europe was over, for those still fighting the Japanese in the South Pacific, it was still far from over, and would continue until August.

Liverpool became the location of the Western Approaches during the Second World War and from here the Battle of the Atlantic was co-ordinated. Without the great ships braving the waves in mighty convoys, at huge risk from German U Boats, to transport food to this island, the people of Britain would have been starved into submission. Author's collection

8 Modern Liverpool

Throughout the late-forties, and into the fifties, the people of Liverpool would attempt to rebuild, both their lives and their city. During the fifty years or so since the ending of the Second World War, Liverpool has witnessed many changes, in terms of culture, attitude, employment, poverty and depression. Large and once dominant industries have lost control over employment trends – the docks, once the largest employer in Liverpool, have been significantly down-sized through the years. And in their place smaller, more productive companies, specialising in technology and the service industry attempt to fill the void.

Liverpool's famous 'Three Graces' in the following three pictures are an instantly recognisable image around the world, and have been since the early years of the twentieth century. But now, in the first decade of the twenty-first century, there are plans to construct a fourth grace: the Liverpool Cloud, *by architect Will Alsop. Should this be allowed? Should something as beautiful as the Three Graces be irreversibly changed with the addition of a modern, futuristic neighbour? It is something that has divided public opinion within Liverpool, and has proved a bone of contention to many purists. Whether or not the people of Liverpool will grow to love a Fourth Grace, only time will tell.* Author's collection

Cunard Line Offices, Pier Head Liverpool

Housing

In the years following the Second World War, Liverpool City Council looked to solve the poor housing in and around the city. In the mid 1950s, the terrace houses along Scotland Road (and many more streets running off there) were earmarked for demolition, to make way for the construction of a new road, and the community that had lived there was scattered throughout the area. New council house estates were built in areas such as Childwall and Woolton and the surrounding areas: a trend that was continued into the middle of the century. New housing required more space, and Liverpool's boundaries were extended again during the 1950s, with much of Hale coming under the control of Liverpool City Council.

In stark contrast to the population explosions of Liverpool's early history, the twentieth century witnessed a gradual decline in the local population. By the 1920s, Liverpool's population had reached an all-time high of around 800,00; yet by the middle of the century a decline had already begun and would continue; by the end of the century Liverpool's population was down to just under 500,000. This pattern is not exclusive to Liverpool, and can be seen right across the North West, and indeed other parts of the country. An explanation is the construction of out-of-town housing; during the early decades of the twentieth century, the Council demolished large areas of the city centre, moving people out to surrounding areas. Vast housing estates were created at Norris Green, Woolton, Kirkby and West Derby, totalling almost 40,000 new homes. Throughout the 1960s, and early 1970s, Labour Governments continued the council house building programmes: by the mid 1970s Liverpool had more than 100,000 council owned houses. Although these were built with the best of intentions, high-rise flats proved not to be the answer, examples such as Cantrill Farm, Tuebrook and Kirkby echo this statement.

By the late 1960s and early 1970s, the new breed of town planner looked to create a series of 'new towns' in the north west to solve the problems of inner-city overcrowding. The village of Kirkby, on the outskirts of Liverpool, became a case in point, and was transformed into a satellite town, expanding beyond all recognition, and home to around 50,000 residents. It became the setting of the fictitious location of Newtown in the *Z Cars* police series, which did little for the town's credibility! Skelmersdale was another such transformation; work began in 1964 to create another new town for West Lancashire, taking between fifty and seventy thousand people from Liverpool's suburbs by the end of the decade.

The appointment of Michael Heseltine as Minister for Merseyside

Liverpool's famous Lime Street: a street as synonymous to Liverpool as its ferries. This picture, taken during the 1950s, depicts the New Empire *and the* North Western Hotel. Author's collection

following the Toxteth riots saw massive investment pour into Liverpool's worst housing estates: Cantrill Farm was redeveloped as Stockbridge Village, for example. In more recent decades the change from council housing to that of housing associations has begun to see steady improvements in the quality of housing for rent. Regeneration of inner-city housing has become the by-word in more recent years, and central Liverpool has benefited from the creation of the Urban Regeneration Strategy: a five year plan, concentrating its efforts on the twenty-two most deprived areas of the borough, it has proved a great success, not just rejuvenating housing, but local amenities, and making a much better environment in which to live and bring up families. Work with the long-term unemployed in these most deprived areas, has helped to restore the confidence that had been lost. Kensington, an area located to the east of the city, has benefited from the New Deal for Communities project pioneered by the New Labour government, with £30 million investment.

And yet, Liverpool housing today is something of a contrast, for despite all that has been done to improve housing in and around Liverpool, there is still a great deal to be done. In 2002, Liverpool City Council admitted that there are still around 25,000 council homes desperately in need of repair and modernisation. And yet, inner-city living is on the increase, with luxury developments from the likes of *Urban Splash* and *Space* being sought after residences.

The Swinging Sixties and the Mersey Beat Sound

The swinging sixties were a period when the people let their hair down, and a period of modern history that witnessed a great revival of Liverpool on the global stage. The inspiration of American pop idols, such as Elvis Presley and Buddy Holly, so impressionable on the British youth of the 1950s, led to a boom in the creation of singers and pop groups by the early sixties. This phenomenon rippled throughout the nation during that influential decade, but never more

The Cavern Pub, *Matthew Street. The Swinging Sixties was a time when Liverpool rocked the world with the Mersey Beat. Undoubtedly the most famous band ever to come out of Liverpool was the Beatles, and their legacy lives on in the city even today.* The Author

so than in Liverpool, with the city becoming the very hub of pop-activity, with performers appearing at a rather dim and grimy basement venue on Matthew Street, known as *The Cavern,* few could have realised that this was to develop into the 'Mersey Beat Sound'. And yet, within a short period of time a host of top bands had formed, whose music would have such a massive influence on pop music, both now and then.

Four young Liverpool men – John Lennon, Paul McCartney, Ringo Starr and George Harrison – would become the Beatles, and from their first debut at *The Cavern* in 1961, their music would rock the world. Songs like *Eleanor Rigby, Strawberry Fields Forever,* and *Penny Lane,* would create pictures and images in the minds of fans around the world of what 1960s Liverpool was all about (as would Gerry Marsden's Pacemakers, with their classic hit *Ferry Across the Mersey).* This heritage still lives on in Liverpool today, the old Cavern Club has been restored and attracts many visitors, as does The Beatles Story at the Albert Dock; Paul McCartney's old terraced house, 40 Forthlin Road, Allerton was purchased by the National Trust as a property worth preserving; and the gates of Strawberry Field, Beaconsfield Road, Woolton have become a shrine to Beatles' fans the world over.

Liverpool created the Beatles, all four members had been born within its boundaries: George Harrison, in Wavertree in 1943, Paul McCartney in Walton Hospital in 1942, John Lennon in Oxford Street Maternity Hospital in 1940, and Ringo Starr in the Dingle in 1940. The city had honoured their ability and revelled in their fame. The Fab Four put the city on top, though its often been said that the fifth Beatle was indeed Liverpool itself. And the city mourned the loss of John Lennon, assassinated in New York, on 8 December, 1980: to commemorate the passing of Liverpool's favourite son, a twenty-four hour vigil was held in the city centre, with a crowd estimated at around 100,000, where a 'ten minute silence' was held. And the people of Liverpool mourned again, on 30 November 2002, when George Harrison lost his battle with cancer.

Cilla Black is another famous Liverpudlian of the 1960s. Born Precilla Marie White, on 27 May 1943, she grew up living above Murray's barber shop on Scotland Road, with her three brothers, George, John and Allen. Education at St Anthony's School in Newsham Street, before later attending Anfield Commercial College, where she studied typing, she began her working career at the BICC in the offices in Liverpool; and in the evening worked as a hat-check

Queen Victoria's Monument stands proudly in Derby Square, on the former site of the castle and later St George's Church, and is one of those landmarks in this busy city that visitors use to meet up with friends and loved ones: 'I'll meet you at Victoria's statue'. Author's collection

girl in the famous Cavern Club, where she was noticed by Beatles manager, Brian Espstein, who offered her a record deal and released her first single in 1963. With hits such as *Step Inside Love* and *You're My World*, Cilla enjoyed a successful singing career, before moving into television by the early 1970s. In more recent years she has become famous for *Surprise, Surprise* and, of course, *Blind Date*.

Changes in Local Government

In 1974, Liverpool parted company with Lancashire. Changes in local government saw the creation of the Metropolitan County of Merseyside, containing five Metropolitan Boroughs: Liverpool, Sefton, Wirral, Knowsley and St Helens. Although this was broadly welcomed by some Liverpool people, it was condemned by others who deeply resented being taken out of their traditional Lancashire. The creation of these new, smaller Metropolitan counties – Greater Manchester as much as Merseyside – seemed to highlight all of the region's problems, such as poverty, unemployment, poor housing and crime, and brought little in the way of benefits. Judged purely on a national level, regions such as Merseyside and Greater Manchester, were soon seen in a very poor light, whereas the more leafy traditional counties, such as Lancashire and Cheshire, with perhaps just as many 'problem areas' were seen as being much more respectable in comparison. Despite campaigns to return to Lancashire, and even though the metropolitan counties were dissolved in 1986, the situation remains unaltered!

Difficult Times

Although the 1960s had witnessed a rise in industrial action, it was a period of prosperity for Liverpool – Fords opened at Halewood in 1962 creating hundreds of jobs, for instance. However, the change in county status seemed all the more unacceptable when it coincided with a significant downturn in the economy. With a massive increase in the level of inflation, and a similarly massive rise in unemployment, industrial action followed.

The downturn was felt in Liverpool. Although traffic using Liverpool's docks had been declining since the 1920s, the pattern seemed to take on a more drastic role by the early 1970s, as more and more docks closed (yet, ironically, Liverpool was still the country's third largest port). The pattern of decline, redundancy and dereliction continued: the workforce was cut by half between the decades of the 1970s and 80s. To attempt to reduce the decline in local industry, Merseyside was made a Development Area in 1969, though with little real success.

Liverpool was looking jaded. By the late 1960s, the showpiece Albert Dock was becoming increasingly redundant and closed in 1972; within a short period of time the complex was derelict, its docks had silted up, and the massive array of warehousing was empty, decaying and looked fit for demolition. And yet, by the 1980s Albert Dock was seen in a whole new light, as a potential new project for the developers. Following in the success that had been achieved in redeveloping the derelict London Docklands, the Isle of Dogs and Canary Wharf, plans were unveiled to do the same to these old now redundant warehouses on the Liverpool waterfront. And yet the very

Images of Liverpool. These two very different picture postcards offer a varied selection of Liverpool landmarks, including the tunnel, The Three Graces, and the Catholic Cathedral, more commonly referred to as the Liverpool Funnel, or Paddy's Wigwam. Author's collection

suggestion that they could be revamped and changed into desirable apartments and shopping complex was met with scepticism and derision locally.

The second half of the 1970s seemed to get worse rather than better. It was a period seemingly filled with strike after strike, culminating in the 'Winter of Discontent' between 1978-9. Within Liverpool, it seemed as though everyone was on strike at sometime: the dockers, the breadmen, the binmen, even the undertakers.

The fall of the Labour Government and the rise of Thatcherism in the following decade led to greater resentment on Merseyside and in Liverpool in particular: whereas its neighbour and arch rival, Manchester, seemed to prosper, Liverpool seemed to enter a deeper period of decline. In the media, Liverpool was painted as the problem city; the city of militancy, strikes, deprivation, unemployment, and crime. It was a desperate and disturbing picture, and one that would have been hard to reverse even with a city council that wanted to change the city's image – however, in Liverpool's case, the city council seemingly had no such intention.

Acts of frustration manifested themselves in many forms: the disastrous Toxteth Riots of 1981 was just one of them. Liverpool was seen in a terrible light, with television showing scenes of running battles on Upper Parliament Street between police and protesters, where petrol bombs were thrown, shops looted and, perhaps most disturbing of all, CS gas deployed on the UK mainland for the first time. Such scenes shocked the nation, and even the seemingly uncaring Conservative Government had to take note of Liverpool's problems.

Following the riots things began to change on Merseyside. Michael Heseltine MP, was appointed with the rather dubious position as Minister for Merseyside by Margaret Thatcher, which unleashed special funding in a new initiative designed to create a new look for Liverpool. The Merseyside Development Corporation was formed, and with its chairman, Leslie Young, strove not just to redevelop Liverpool, but to change its national image. They achieved at great deal in a very short space of time. In 1984, the International Garden Festival was held at Riverside just outside the city centre, with exhibits from twenty-eight countries, officially opened by HM Queen Elizabeth II and the Duke of Edinburgh. Together with the Tall Ships Race, held in the River Mersey between 1-4 August, these events attracted crowds of people to the Liverpool waterfront. It was a tiny step in the right direction. Investment continued, which led to the redevelopment of the derelict docklands.

Politically, with the divisions in the Labour Party widening, Liverpool witnessed the rise of the Militant Tendency. The City Council became controlled by this radical breed of Labour activist. Run by Deputy Leader, Derek Hatton, the City Council pursued its own left-wing agenda. Matters came to a head in 1985, when the council refused to set a rate, and over one hundred Labour councillors were removed from office. The Labour Party, now led by Neil Kinnock, took on the Militants, with great effect, famously in his Bournemouth conference speech that year in which he condemned them as being 'a Labour Council, hiring taxis to scurry around the city, handing out redundancy notices to council workers'. Eric Heffer, Liverpool Walton MP, and Derek Hatton walked out of the conference centre in protest. Militant, as a credible political movement, began losing its voice in Liverpool from that period onwards, and within two years had lost any control it had over Liverpool City Council. By 1990, following the removal of Margaret Thatcher as Prime Minister, the movement lost its primary target, and it seemed to lose its political cause too.

In the wake of Hatton and the Militant Tendency, the City Council was controlled by more traditional and stable Labour leaders, including Coombes and Rimmer. However, growing dissatisfaction with the Labour run city council during the 1990s witnessed a back-lash by 1998 and the intervention of a Liberal Democrat run council instead, led by Councillor Mike Story. Although the Lib-Dems had been on the rise in Liverpool since the days of the Alliance, it was still quite a surprise to see them take control of a Council that has always been regarded as a safe Labour stronghold. Moreover, despite their critics – who claimed that this was some minor political process, and Labour would surely retake control of the council at a forthcoming election – the Lib-Dems have retained control of Liverpool City Council, by delivering what the voters wanted them to deliver: improved services.

The Arrival Of His Eminence The Pope

The planned arrival of Pope John Paul II had aroused great feeling both in Liverpool and throughout Merseyside, and fed an underlying degree of sectarianism that existed within the city. Amongst Liverpool's Catholics, this visit was something really special, something beyond words... history in the making... and was met with great jubilation. To Liverpool's Protestants, this visit meant nothing special, and was met with some derision: throughout the city graffiti appeared saying 'Remember 1689', 'No surrender' and 'No Pope Here'. Some of this emotive graffiti still exists in the city to present day – just outside Edge Hill Station, a wall, easily seen from the train, still reads 'No Pope Here', for example.

Pope John Paul's plane touched down at Speke Airport on 30 May, 1982, met by massive crowds that had gathered at the airport to welcome his arrival. Massive crowds, of many faiths, lined the streets, to catch a glimpse of His Eminence, in his now legendary 'Popemobile'. Through the years, Liverpool's Catholic and Protestant communities had endeavoured to form closer ties, largely due to the good working relationship of Archbishop Warlock and Bishop Sheppard, and as a sign of acceptance, the Pope visited Liverpool's Anglican Cathedral, where he was greeted by Bishop David Sheppard, Cardinal Hulme and Archbishop Worlock. Despite the attitude of some of Liverpool's Protestant community prior to the Pope's arrival in the UK, he received a truly warm welcome here, the choir sang and the congregation applauded his entrance. From there he continued his journey to the Metropolitan Cathedral, were he held communion. Although the Pope only remained in the city for one day, it is estimated that more than one million people had come out on to the streets to see him. The following morning he re-boarded his plane at Speke Airport, and departed Liverpool to continue his historic tour of the nation.

A Pool of Talent

Liverpool has always been a city of natural, home-grown culture and talent. Although the spotlight shone bright on the city during the Mersey Beat era, before and after that period, Liverpool has created some talented performers. It is a city noted for its natural humour and has created many comedians, including Arthur Askey, Jimmy Tarbuck, Tom O'Conner and Maurice Cole (better known as Kenny Everett). Its television personalities, such as Frankie Vaughan, Cilla Black, Ken Dodd (and his Diddy men, who made the Liverpool suburb of Knotty Ash famous) and Les Dennis. Writers, such as Willy Russell, Beryl Bainbridge, Alan Bleasdale (renowned for his gritty dramas like *Boys from the Black Stuff*) and Carla Lane (with Scouse sitcoms like, *The Liver Birds* and *Bread*), have never forgotten their Liverpool roots. And talented actors like Michael Angelis, Tom Bell, the former *Doctor Who* Tom Baker, the *Royle Family's* Ricky Tomlinson, and who can forget Geoffrey Hughes, as *Coronation Street's* loveable Scouse rogue, Eddy Yates? In more recent years, however, Phil Redmond's *Brookside* has become synonymous with life in Liverpool and on Merseyside. Liverpool has been linked with pop music since the days of the Mersey Beat, and that image lives on today with the likes of former Spice Girl Mel C and Atomic Kitten.

The city's outstanding collection of classic and historic buildings, such as the docklands and the Victorian and Georgian terraces – Falkner Terrace on Upper Parliament Street and Mornington Terrace on Upper Duke Street are two good examples of the type of architecture – have made Liverpool an ideal setting for filming of some of the period dramas in recent years, such as the BBC's rendition of Charles Dickens' classic tale *David Copperfield;* Windermere Terrace was used as a location for ITV's *Forsyte Saga* in 2001. Filming in the city continues to grow, and aids the local economy.

Soccer on Merseyside: the Blues and the Reds

With the end of the war came the reinstatement of the Football League, and both the players and the fans were eager to get started once more. Liverpool's two clubs, took up where they had left off, as arch rivals. And Liverpool won the 1947 Football League Championship, to even up the fact that Everton had won the last before the war.

Fortunes changed during the years of the 1960s and 1970s, when both clubs won the FA Cup and other titles. Of the two clubs, however, Liverpool were always viewed as 'the club', and Everton the 'underdogs'. Under the leadership of Bill Shankly, Liverpool FC would seemingly rule football, not just in Britain, but in Europe too. During the eighties, however, despite success on the pitch, the club, its fans, and the people of Liverpool, were deeply affected by the disasters of Heysel and Hillsborough.

Liverpool met Juventus FC at the Heysel Stadium in Brussels, on 29 May, 1985 for the final of the European Cup. However, the match was never completed, for things turned ugly prior to the kick-off, with fighting on the terraces between rival fans: what began as a fight soon turned into a riot, as the seats were ripped out and used as missiles. The dividing fence between the two sides was breached by the Liverpool fans, and as the Juventus fans attempted to flee, the weight of people brought a wall down upon them. In total thirty-nine people were killed, the majority of which were Italians. Liverpool fans were blamed for the horrific incident, which was covered in graphic detail by both television and the media in general. Eventually, following a lengthy investigation, run jointly by

Hillsborough Oaks was created from an idea by Charles Davis: ninety-six oak trees were planted on a plot of land off Netherley Road, one for each of the fans that lost their lives on 15 April 1989 at the Hillsborough Stadium. The memorial garden was officially opened by Councillor James Keight OBE JP, leader of Knowsley Council, on 29 September 2000. Bulbs were planted by Nottingham City Council on 18 November 2001, to signify the sympathy of the people of Nottingham. The Author

the British and Belgian police, the culprits were arrested. For Liverpool FC it meant shame: Joe Fagan resigned as manager. For the FA it meant that all English clubs were banned from playing in Europe.

However, further tragedy was just around the corner. The 1988-89 season had also begun well for the club, and they had gained many victories. By the time they met Nottingham Forest FC at Hillsborough, Liverpool were top of the League. The disaster that occurred here has been covered in great detail through the years, and it is perhaps not fitting to dredge through it all again. Suffice it to say that on that day what occurred resulted in the death of ninety-six fans, having been crushed into a small enclosure. Who was to blame? Yorkshire Police for opening the gates at the Leppings Lane end, allowing the fans to surge into and along the narrow tunnel? The fans themselves for rushing in, eager to see the match, which by this time had already begun? Or the security fencing that had been erected at all grounds to prevent pitch invasion (which in this case prevented their escape)? Elements of all three, or was it just a tragic accident? It is not for me to judge.

The scenes, just as at Heysel, were covered by the media. As soon as news of the tragedy broke, people began to gather at the Shankly Gates outside Anfield, leaving flowers, cards, scarves and other sentimental gifts. On the Sunday massive crowds came to the Memorial Service held at Anfield, attended by the Liverpool team, and Prince Charles: flowers were laid on the pitch and a minutes silence was held, when the whole of the city fell silent. The club, the league and the country mourned what had occurred that day at Hillsborough, and vowed it would never occur again. In the years that have followed the tragedy, the families still continue to fight for justice for the ninety-six that died.

Following the successes on the pitch during the 1980s, the following decade saw almost a complete reversal of fortunes. However, in more recent years, the club has witnessed much greater success again, under the management of Gerrard Houllier, and with immensely talented stars – such as Michael Owen, taking the club to the top once more. And so too have their arch-rivals Everton. It has been some time since Everton have been placed near the top of the Premiership, but in the 2002/3 season, following the appointment of David Moyes as manager from Preston North End, and the talents of their new young striker, Wayne Rooney, the team is battling with its old rival for the top of the table once more.

The motorway age arrived in 1959 with the opening of the Preston Bypass, and soon other motorways were planned. Liverpool joined the motorway revolution in the late 1970s with the opening of M62 motorway, connecting it to Manchester and across the Pennines to Yorkshire. The Author

The Post-War Road Building Boom

Although the opening of the East Lancashire Road had initially eased congestion and significantly shortened the travelling time between Liverpool and Manchester, by the 1950s, traffic had risen to a point where the road was no-longer doing the job it had been intended. During the 1960s, to remedy this problem, at least in the short term, the East Lancashire Road was made wider throughout its length, into a double lane, dual carriageway.

Since the late-1940s, there had been the suggestion of creating a super highway, to connect Lancashire and Yorkshire: in fact, soon after the East Lancashire Road had been completed, there were thoughts of extending it through to Yorkshire, but the Second World War intervened and plans were mothballed. With traffic increasing, a new highway was planned; the driving force behind Lancashire's motorway network was James Drake, its chief surveyor, who had a vision of super highways. The success of the Preston Bypass, had seen it transformed into the country's first motorway, handling the flow of traffic between the north and south. Drake now proposed another to cross the country west to east, linking Lancashire with Yorkshire. The new highway – which was to become the M62 motorway – was built in sections, as relief by-pass roads: the first of these was built in Eccles in 1969, followed by sections in Liverpool, and eventually joined by the middle section passing St Helens, Burtonwood and Winwick, built in 1973, with the completed motorway opening in November 1976.

Work on the M62 was not alone. Liverpool desperately needed an inner link road. Although this had been planned for construction as early as 1964, work did not commence until March 1967. Despite this delay, the work was completed on time and opened to traffic during the summer of 1971; called the M53, it was known locally as the Inner Liverpool Motorway. The success of these new highways led to the creation of the M58, connecting Liverpool to Wigan and the M6.

A Period of Regeneration

For many years, Liverpool was seen as the forgotten North-West city: a city left to linger in the past, filled with old and often decaying buildings. When compared to its more vibrant neighbour, Manchester, Liverpool looked old and jaded.

Following the turmoil of the early 1980s, Liverpool was in dire need of re-generation. It was an ailing city that was showing its age. Its once glorious docklands were looking tired. Warehouses that were once filled to the roof with goods from around the world, now stood empty and derelict. Liverpool's once magnificent waterfront had become a real eyesore. However, with investment and an undying determination to achieve the unthinkable, things can indeed be turned around.

The Merseyside Development Corporation worked in earnest to redevelop the waterfront. Albert Dock, built in 1846 by Jesse Hartley, had been in such a poor state that the intention had been to simply

St John's Gardens & Entrance to Mersey Tunnel, Liverpool.   G 2755

St John's Garden, at the rear of St George's Hall, is a small piece of green in an ever-increasing city centre. It is an ideal place to sit, relax, watch the world pass by, or just eat your lunch. Author's collection

demolish this Victorian eyesore; it was instead completely reconstructed at a cost of almost £100 million. This was a huge transformation, changing it from an ageing warehouse to a centre used for both commercial and residential purposes. The Merseyside Development Corporation, the driving force behind the transformation, won the 1986 European Gold Medal Award for the restoration of historic monuments and buildings for the conservation work they had carried out at the Albert Dock, and the results they achieved. The complex, which is the country's largest Grade I building, now comprises the Tate Gallery, shopping facilities, offices and over one hundred luxury apartments, was officially opened on 24 May 1988 by HRH Prince Charles. In the following year, the Tate Gallery was voted Fine Art Museum of the Year, and in the November Princess Margaret visited Albert Dock to open the new Maritime Museum.

Parker Street gently guides visitors from Lime Street Station into the busy city centre streets of Church Street and Lord Street. Just compare these two images, one taken during the 1930s and the other in 2003. Author's collection

The Albert Dock, the country's largest Grade I listed building, was refurbished in 1986 at a cost of £100 million, and was officially opened on 24 May 1988 by HRH Prince Charles. Comprising of the Merseyside Maritime Museum, the Tate Gallery, shopping facilities, offices and over one hundred luxury apartments, today it is one of the region's most popular tourist attractions. The Author

The focus returned to Liverpool's waterfront again in the early 1990s. The Tall Ships returned to Liverpool's waterfront again in August 1992, and Liverpool's vital role as the premiere western port during the Second World War was recalled during the Commemoration of the Battle of the Atlantic held in May of 1993.

In more recent years, Liverpool city centre has witnessed massive investment for regeneration schemes. St John's Market, originally built in 1822, received a massive makeover in concrete during the late-1960s and early 1970s, with the addition of the 450 foot high St John's Beacon, has seen massive refurbishment again in recent years. The centre of Liverpool has been transformed with the many streets, including Church Street and Parker Street, becoming pedestrianised, and the opening of new stores and precincts has uplifted the city centre, making it a more attractive place in which to shop.

Not prepared to rest on their laurels, the City Council has other schemes planned, including the proposed regeneration of Paradise Street and Canning Place. This proposal has endured some delays and setbacks. The original proposed redevelopment of Chavasse Park, by the Walton Group in 1996, would be rejected by the Deputy Prime Minister, John Prescott in June 2002. This opened the way for a rival bid from Grosvenor Henderson to go before the Council's Planning Committee.

Although St John's Market dates from the late Georgian era, most people think of the concrete precinct created during the late-1960s and early 1970s, with the addition of the 450 foot high St John's Beacon. One of Liverpool's most prominent landmarks, the Beacon once had a revolving restaurant - today it is home to Radio City and Liverpool's Magic . The Author

In recent years Liverpool has begun to transform its appearance. Its once dowdy looking streets have been given a facelift and are bustling with people, as seen here in Church Street. And, trendy wine bars are opening throughout the city, as here in Queens Square. The Author

Although Liverpool has come a long way in recent years, there is still much to be done. Within the next few years, Grosvenor Henderson intend to develop the area around Hanover Street, Peter Street, Paradise Street, South John Street and Chavasse Park; the aging bus station will be demolished, along with other old and decaying buildings, to clear the way for the creation of a £700 million complex, consisting of retail, leisure and residential facilities.

The Author

Grosvenor Henderson intend to develop the 43 acre site – which covers Hanover Street, Peter Street, Paradise Street, South John Street and Chavasse Park – to create a £700 million complex suited for a combination of retail, leisure and residential purposes. As part of the changes, the *Queen's Moat House Hotel* will have to be demolished, but will be replaced with a much larger hotel on Hanover Street. If the work does go-ahead, it will transform one of the most rundown areas of Liverpool's centre, and in the process, create almost 5000 jobs.

And a further boost to public transport within Liverpool was announced by the Transport Secretary, Alistair Darling, on 11 December 2002: Liverpool will be granted £170 million to introduce a tram system, similar to Manchester Metrolink, which is hoped to be operational by 2007.

Today, Liverpool is a rejuvenated and vibrant city. Of course it has its problems – what city doesn't, but it is learning to deal with them. Sadly, in Liverpool's case, its problems are more often than not exaggerated by the media: at the start of the new millennium, a national crime survey placed Liverpool outside the top twenty towns and cities, yet the media insists on portraying Liverpool as hot spot of criminality. Within the city centre, building, redevelopment and investment are at an all-time high. After a great many years Liverpool has a fresh feel about itself. Liverpool has a bright future in the twenty-first century.

*E*PILOGUE

Liverpool's story has been one of continuous change. It has witnessed periods of great prosperity: its port was once the envy of the maritime world, handling huge ships with cargoes from all over the world, whose profits were used to create the city's classical architecture. It has witnessed periods of decline, poverty, mass unemployment, deprivation and neglect, particularly during the Thatcher years of the 1980s. And yet the city has weathered the storm, and now looks forward with great hope to the future.

The people of Liverpool celebrated the dawn of the new millennium. Liverpool City Council and the events organisers really 'pushed the boat out' for New Years Eve 1999, with massive celebrations throughout the city. The main event was located on Liverpool's world-famous waterfront, with live music, parties and a massive fireworks and laser display projected on to the Three Graces and across the river. It was a spectacular once-in-a-lifetime event, reputed to be the biggest organised Millennium event outside of London, and the people celebrated and partied long into the night. The new century was surely to bring only the very best to Liverpool and its inhabitants.

Liverpool's world-famous waterfront is about to change its appearance, for to prove that the city is still moving with the times, a 'Fourth Grace' has been commissioned. Leading architects placed bids – all of which were controversial – offering to create a truly modern piece of architecture to stand alongside the three more traditional buildings. The decision led to much local debate: should anyone meddle with such an instantly recognisable waterfront? Of the four design's that were short listed, the public's favourite (or should that be least offensive?) was Sir Norman Foster's *Ship*, which embraced Liverpool's maritime heritage. However, the panel of judges came to another conclusion, and when the winner was announced by Sir Joe Dywer, chairman of Liverpool Vision, on 6 December 2002, the winning bid went to Will Alsop's *Liverpool Cloud*, which had been described by many in the city as a cross between a spaceship and a huge donut! Construction work is scheduled to commence in 2005, with a proposed completion date of 2007, to celebrate Liverpool's 800th anniversary.

Further alterations to the waterfront are planned. Liverpool City Council, Liverpool Vision and Everton FC created a partnership to

The Mona Lennon: *a huge image of Liverpool's favourite son, the late John Lennon, in the guise of the Mona Lisa - currently displayed on the façade of St George's Hall - offered proof that, although the city took its bid to become the European Capital of Culture 2008 very seriously, it was still prepared to make fun of itself!* The Author

regenerate the King's Dock, proposing the construction of a new super-stadium, and many other leisure and tourist facilities. This redevelopment is a lavish proposal, using both public and private investment, with an estimated price tag of around £300 million – of which £65 million would have to be generated by Everton Football Club. However, these plans have proved controversial, and led to many heated debates.

Although Everton was the preferred choice to host this new development, with an impressive new stadium, constant delays and the inability to deliver the estimated capital injection required to make the stadium a reality, led to Everton losing its preferred status in December 2002. Further meetings continued between Liverpool Vision and Everton into the new year, in order to put things back on track, however, despite much effort from both sides, it was announced on 28 February that Everton would be withdrawing from the King's Dock Development, and looking to construct a new stadium elsewhere in the city. Although this has been a huge blow to Liverpool Visions' plans for the King's Dock, redevelopment will still take place with other proposals being formulated.

Liverpool's regeneration in recent years has been rapid. The image of the old and decaying city has been swept away and replaced with one that reflects the modern Liverpool – the Liverpool of the twenty-first century. To seal Liverpool's regeneration, the City Council bid for the coveted prize of *European Capital of Culture 2008*, and made the short list, along with Bristol, Newcastle/Gateshead, Birmingham, Oxford and Cardiff. Liverpool has for many years been the home of culture, this is reflected in its galleries, its theatres, its school of performing arts, its actors, writers, singers and musicians, its architecture, and its classic waterfront, which is to become a *World Heritage Site*. But to impress the judges, Liverpool would have to prove that it truly deserves to be the *European Capital of Culture*. One new addition to Liverpool's cultural character is FACT, a modern museum dedicated to the moving image, which cost £10 million. Located in the rejuvenated old tea factory, it opened its doors to the media and a host of celebrities from the art world on 20 February, including Sir Bob Scott, director of Liverpool's Capital of Culture Bid, who was very impressed. The public were allowed inside two days later, and initial reactions have been both enthusiastic and positive. In an effort to woo supporters, Liverpool City Council held a reception on the terrace of the House of Commons on 3 March, where a host of celebrities and key players were invited. The event, which projected Liverpool as a city reborn, featured the strange image referred to as the *Mona Lennon*: a painting of Liverpool's favourite son, the late John Lennon, in the guise of the Mona Lisa – perhaps proving that although the city takes the bid very seriously, it is still prepared to make fun of itself!

Although Liverpool was one of the favourites (along with Newcastle/Gateshead and Birmingham), it came second to Newcastle/Gateshead during the BBC's *Clash of the Cities* poll. The ultimate decision would be made by the special committee of judges, and announced on 4 June. The Liverpool Bid team gathered early that morning and waited nervously for the decision. At 8.10 am Tessa Jowell, the Culture Secretary, gave the announcement: the competition had been 'of the highest standard' and Liverpool had won! Spontaneous celebration erupted right across the city. The *Liverpool Echo's* front page summoned it up: 'WE DID IT!' Sir Bob Scott commented that 'for the first time for too long Liverpool will represent Great Britain' and added 'Hopefully Liverpool will be the best capital of culture ever!'

Securing the prize will ensure £millions of investment for Liverpool – Glasgow benefited immensely as European Capital of Culture 1990 – bringing much needed employment. The city will celebrate its achievement for the next five years, and yet there is still a great deal of work to be done. In 2007, Liverpool will celebrate 800 years of existence on the banks of the River Mersey. It has been an interesting, and at times demanding, journey. Huge celebrations are planned to celebrate this most significant anniversary – which will be all the more enjoyable now that Liverpool has secured the title *European Capital of Culture 2008*.

And what of Liverpool's future? Right now, in the infant years of the twenty-first century, Liverpool is enjoying a revival; the period of renaissance of the last few years has seen massive reinvestment on the city, its infrastructure and its architecture. The city is buzzing with excitement: speak to the people of Liverpool and it is obvious that the optimism that has been missing for many years has returned – they have real pride in the city once more. Liverpool today, has all the charm and charisma of the Mersey Beat days, when Liverpool was the place to be; and the commerce and investment of the late-nineteenth century. That's definitely a world-beating combination!

The ancient 'wishing gate', Liverpool. Author's collection

$\mathcal{S}$ELECT BIBLIOGRAPHY

Anderson, Paul, *An Illustrated History of Liverpool's Railways* (Irwell Press, 1996).

Aughton, Peter, *Liverpool: A People's History* (Carnegie Press, 1990).

Bagley, J J, *A History of Lancashire* (Phillimore, 1976).

Beamont, William, *A Discourse of the Civil Warr in Lancashire* (Chetham Society, volume 62, 1864).

Bolt, Geoffrey, *A Regional History of the Railways of Gt. Britain: Vol 10, The North West* (David & Charles, 1978).

Box, Charles E, *The Liverpool Overhead Railway* (Ian Allan Ltd, London, 1984).

Broxap, Ernest, *The Great Civil War in Lancashire* (Manchester University Press, 1910).

Chandler, George, *An Illustrated History of Liverpool* (Rondo Publications, 1972).

Chandler, George, *Liverpool* (Batsford, 1957).

Chandler, George, *Liverpool Shipping, A Short History* (Phoenix House, London, 1960).

Cockcroft, W R, *The Albert Dock and Liverpool's Historic Waterfront* (Print Origination, 1994).

Crosby, Alan, *A History of Lancashire* (Phillimore, 1995).

Curtis, John, *Liverpool* (Jarrod Publishing, 2002).

Edwards, B J N, *Vikings in North West England* (University of Lancaster, 1998).

Hadfield, Charles and Gordon Biddle, *The Canals of North West England* (David & Charles, 1970).

Hayes, Cliff, *The Changing Face of Merseyside* (Breedon Books, 2002).

Horne, J B and T B Maund, *Liverpool Transport, Volume 1.* (Senior Publications, 1975).

Hughes, Quentin, Seaport, *Architecture & Townscape in Liverpool* (Lund Humphries 1969).

Hyde, Francis E, *Liverpool & The Mersey, The Development of a Port, 1700-1970* (David & Charles 1971).

Joyce, J, *Roads, Rails and Ferries of Liverpool* (Ian Allan, 1983).

Kelly, Michael, *The Life and Times of Kitty Wilkinson* (Countrywise, 2000).

Kelly, Stephen F, *Illustrated History Of Liverpool, 1892-1998* (Hamlyn, 1998).

Lamb, Charles L, and Eric Smallpage, *The Story of Liverpool* (*Daily Post*, 1936).

Lancashire County Council: *A Preliminary Plan for Lancashire* (1952).

Lane, Tony, *Liverpool: City of the Sea* (Liverpool University Press, 1987).

McIntyre-Brown, Arabella, and Guy Woodland, *Liverpool, The First 1,000 Years* (Garlic Press, 2001).

Midwinter, E, 'Local Boards of Health in Lancashire' (*Trans. of the Hist. Soc. of Lan. & Ches.* volume 117).

Midwinter, Eric, *Old Liverpool* (David & Charles, 1971).

Moore, Bart, Sir Edward, *Liverpool in King Charles the Second's Time* (Henry Young, 1899).

Muir, R, *A History of Liverpool* (University Press of Liverpool, 1907).

North West Joint Planning Team: *A Strategic Plan for the North West* (1974).

Ormrod, George, *Tracts Relating to the Military Proceedings in Lancashire During the Great Civil War* (Chetham Society, volume 2, 1844).

Northcote-Parkinson, C, *The Rise of the Port of Liverpool* (Liverpool University Press, 1952).

Perrett, Bryan, *Liverpool, A City at War* (Robert Hale, 1990).

Rowland, John, *George Stephenson: Creator of Britain's Railways* (Odhams Press, 1954).

Walker, Brian, and Ann Hinchliffe, *In Our Liverpool Home* (Blackstaff Press, 1978).

Whitworth, Rodney, *Merseyside at War* (Scouse Press, 1988).

$\mathscr{I}$NDEX